METRO & LIGHT RAIL SYSTEMS
SHEFFIELD: FROM TRAM TO
TRAM-TRAIN

Ian Beardsley, Robert Pritchard & Alan Yearsley

Published by Platform 5 Publishing Ltd, 52 Broadfield Road, Sheffield, S8 0XJ, England.

Printed in England by The Amadeus Press, Cleckheaton, West Yorkshire.

ISBN 978 1 909431 76 8

CONTENTS

Front cover (top left): Double deck car 281, built in 1912, is seen on the Abbey Lane reserved track on 22 February 1959. To the right is the final Roberts car 536, new in 1952 and full of enthusiasts on this day touring the system – a week later this route would close. **Howard Turner**

Front cover (top right): Tram-train 399 201 is seen on the Tinsley chord as it passes from the Network Rail tracks onto the Supertram network with a service from Rotherham Parkgate to Sheffield Cathedral on 25 October 2018, the tram-train opening day. **Robert Pritchard**

Front cover (main photo): 107 is seen at the Cathedral stop, in the centre of Sheffield, with a Yellow Route service to Meadowhall on 15 June 2011. **Robert Pritchard**

Back cover: Tram-train 399 203 leaves the Rotherham Parkgate terminus with a service for Cathedral on 3 February 2019. **Robert Pritchard**

Right: Reflecting on a successful first 25 years?: In this publication every one of Sheffield current fleet of 32 Siemens trams and Stadler tram-trains are illustrated at least once! On 30 November 2019 car 115 runs above the Sheffield & Tinsley Canal on the approach to the Attercliffe stop operating an early afternoon Yellow Route service from Meadowhall to Middlewood. **Robert Pritchard**

25 years ago, in 1995, Platform 5 Published "Tram to Supertram – An old friend returns to the streets of Sheffield" to celebrate the opening of the Supertram system. A few copies of this special publication are still available from Platform 5 Publishing, price £4.95.

INTRODUCTION

It is now 25 years since the opening of the Sheffield Supertram system and the publication of Platform 5's popular Tram to Supertram book. Since then Supertram has established itself as an invaluable part of Sheffield's public transport network, even if passenger numbers have been lower than anticipated and a number of extensions have been proposed but have not so far materialised. This means that unlike some other light rail networks in the UK, the Supertram system has remained largely unchanged since it opened – apart from the long-held ambition of running tram-trains (the first in the UK) to Rotherham Parkgate, which finally came to fruition in October 2018.

Because of this, now would seem like as good a time as any to compile a present-day guide to the Supertram and tram-train system, its background, history, infrastructure, operations and vehicle fleets. Although the main purpose of this book is to cover the present day tramway, we have also included some historical material on Sheffield's first generation tramway, preserved Sheffield trams, and the rise, fall and renaissance of trams as a form of urban public transport in the UK.

This will be the first in a series of books covering the UK tram and light rail systems: it is planned to produce a similar publication for each network over the next few years.

We hope you will find this book an interesting and useful source of information. It draws on material from a number of earlier Platform 5 publications, including our own UK Metro & Light Rail Systems handbooks, the Platform 5 Tram to Supertram book published in 1995, various editions of the Light Rail Review series published in the late 1980s and 1990s, back copies of **entrain** and **Today's Railways UK** magazines, official Siemens and Supertram literature from the time of the tramway's opening and a number of lectures and technical briefings on the tram-train project.

We have made every effort to ensure that all information is correct at the time of going to press but cannot be held responsible for any errors or omissions. Nonetheless, any corrections or suggestions for improvements for any future editions would be most gratefully received. Any comments on this publication can be addressed to the authors by email at **updates@platform5.com** or by post to the Platform 5 address on the title page.

ACKNOWLEDGEMENTS

Thanks are given to all the individuals who have helped in the compilation of this book. We are particularly indebted to Paul Jackson, who was very closely involved with the project for many years and was one of the original authors of our Tram to Supertram book, for access to his huge archive of slides. Thanks are also due to Howard Turner, Edward Marshall, Andy Barclay, Paul Fox, Paul Abell, Keith Fender, Barry Clark and Tom Robinson for their assistance with sourcing archive material and photographs. If readers have any photos that they would like to be considered for our forthcoming tram system handbooks (particularly any illustrating the early years) please do get in touch using the email **pictures@platform5.com**.

UPDATES

Any major developments with Supertram and tram-train, and the country's other light rail and tram systems, can be found in the magazine **Today's Railways UK**. This is available at all good newsagents or on post-free subscription. Please see the inside covers of this book for further details.

Ian Beardsley, Robert Pritchard & Alan Yearsley. March 2020.

THE RISE, FALL AND RISE AGAIN
OF TRAMWAYS
IN THE UK

Sheffield was the second city in the UK to reintroduce trams in 1994, after the opening of Manchester's Metrolink system in 1992. This marked the start of a tramway renaissance in British cities following a period of almost total abandonment in the decades after World War II.

The UK had the honour of having the world's first passenger railway: the Swansea & Mumbles Railway, opened to passengers in 1807. This was also the world's first passenger tramway, as it used tramway type vehicles throughout its life despite being referred to as a railway. Horse-drawn trams were used for most of the 19th century, although it would be 1860 before the next horse tramway opened in Birkenhead. Many more horse tramways opened in the latter part of the 19th century, and by the 1870s and 1880s some of these were switching from horse to steam traction.

The late 19th and early 20th century also saw some towns and cities such as Edinburgh and Matlock experiment with cable propelled tramways following the example set by San Francisco, USA, with its world-famous cable tramway, which opened in 1873. The Glasgow Subway also used the cable system from its opening in 1896 until 1935. Today, there are no surviving street running cable tramways in the UK apart from the Great Orme Tramway in Llandudno, North Wales. However, strictly speaking this is a funicular rather than a cable tramway, as the cars are stopped and started by stopping and starting the cable, to which they are permanently fixed, unlike a cable tramway where the cable runs continuously and the cars can be attached to and detached from the cable.

In 1885 the UK's first electric tramway opened in Blackpool, following earlier examples of electric traction in the early 1880s such as Sestroretsk in Russia, Lichterfelde, near Berlin, and the Mödling and Hinterbrühl Tram in Austria. Blackpool initially used a conduit electrification system whereby trams collected electric current from a conduit beneath the tracks via a groove between the two running rails. This system was also used on tram lines in central London, but was soon found to be unsuitable for Blackpool because the conduit was frequently damaged by sand and sea water, and it was replaced by overhead wires in 1899.

A few horse tramways had closed by the early 1900s, but most were then converted to electric traction. One notable exception was Morecambe, which operated horse trams from 1887 until 1912 and then petrol trams until closure of the system in 1924. The early 1900s also saw the opening of several completely new electric tramways, including many in small towns such as Ilkeston, Merthyr Tydfil and Weston-super-Mare.

It is often said that the heyday of the electric tram in the UK was between the 1900s and the 1920s. One of the shortest-lived networks in the country was the Sheerness & District Tramways, which ran

Leeds 180 is seen under a threatening sky at the National Tramway Museum at Crich, Derbyshire on 7 November 2015. Visible to the left are outer London area operator Metropolitan Electric Tramways car 331 and Blackpool standard car 40. **Robert Pritchard**

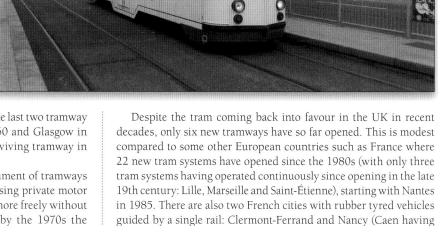

only from 1903 until 1917. Tramway closures began in earnest in the late 1920s, with several more small and medium-sized town networks following suit in the 1930s. By this time tramways were increasingly being replaced by buses and trolleybuses. Notable pre-war closures included Wolverhampton in 1928 and Nottingham in 1936.

In 1949, Manchester was the first major city to abandon its tram network after World War II. Almost all remaining systems then followed suit in the 1950s such as Edinburgh in 1956, Liverpool in 1957, Aberdeen in 1958 and Leeds in 1959. By this time rising levels of car ownership and improvements in the design of motor buses meant that tramways were falling out of favour in the UK and in many other countries such as Canada, France, the USA and Australia. The last two tramway closures in the UK took place in Sheffield in 1960 and Glasgow in 1962, after which Blackpool became the sole surviving tramway in the country.

One of the reasons often cited for the abandonment of tramways was that they caused congestion, and that increasing private motor car traffic meant that cars and buses could move more freely without trams getting in their way. However, already by the 1970s the Government and local authorities began to realise that the car was becoming a victim of its own success and that more radical public transport-based solutions were needed. The UK's first modern light rail system was the Tyne & Wear Metro, opened in 1980, followed by the Docklands Light Railway in 1987. However, these are light metros rather than tramways, as they run entirely on dedicated rights of way (including some tunnel sections) and do not have any street running. After Manchester in 1992 and Sheffield in 1994, a further four new tramways have opened in the UK: Birmingham in 1999, Croydon (2000), Nottingham (2004) and Edinburgh (2014). Of these, Manchester's Metrolink has seen a number of new routes since 2000, and extensions at both ends of the West Midlands Metro line between Birmingham and Wolverhampton have also opened or are under construction. By contrast, Croydon's Tramlink network has remained unchanged, as has the Sheffield Supertram system apart from the tram-train route to Rotherham. A number of other tramway schemes, including the Bristol and Leeds Supertram and Liverpool's Merseytram, have been proposed but abandoned.

Despite the tram coming back into favour in the UK in recent decades, only six new tramways have so far opened. This is modest compared to some other European countries such as France where 22 new tram systems have opened since the 1980s (with only three tram systems having operated continuously since opening in the late 19th century: Lille, Marseille and Saint-Étienne), starting with Nantes in 1985. There are also two French cities with rubber tyred vehicles guided by a single rail: Clermont-Ferrand and Nancy (Caen having also operated such a system until the end of 2017, but this has now been converted to a conventional tramway which opened in July 2019).

Whereas in the post-war period the tram was seen as the cause of road congestion, the private car is now widely regarded as the main cause of this problem and the tram is increasingly coming to be regarded as the solution even if it has been slower to catch on in the UK than elsewhere in Europe. Where traffic signals are properly managed and trams are given priority over other vehicles at road junctions they enjoy a significant advantage over cars and other road users. Trams also have multiple entrances and exits unlike buses, and passengers usually either buy a ticket before boarding or from a conductor during the journey rather than paying the driver as they board, thus reducing dwell times at stops. Although the cost per vehicle is generally higher for a tram than for a bus, the overall cost is cheaper for a tram when the life expectancy of the vehicle is taken into account. Research and experience has also shown that motorists are more likely to be lured out of their cars onto trams than onto buses, with the bus being perceived as a less comfortable and generally less attractive form of transport than the private car or the tram.

SHEFFIELD'S FIRST TRAMS: 87 YEARS OF SERVICE

As with most other tramways in the UK, Sheffield's original tram network started life as a horse tramway. The original routes opened between 1873 and 1877, serving Attercliffe, Brightside, Carbrook, Heeley, Nether Edge and Owlerton, and were constructed under the 1870 Tramways Act. Under the legislation at that time local authorities were not allowed to operate tramways themselves but they did have powers to build them and lease the lines to an individual or to an operating company. In this case the tracks were constructed by contractors for the Sheffield Corporation and leased to the Sheffield Tramways Company, which operated the initial services.

Horse trams gave a smoother ride on their steel rails than the horse buses previously operated, but still charged much higher fares than most ordinary workers could afford. The cost of keeping a large number of horses in stock meant that the tramway company could not offer low fares for workers, who therefore still had to live as close to their workplace as possible and walk to and from work each day. A notable feature of Sheffield horse trams was that each car normally carried a different colour scheme to denote the route to which it was allocated, as well as bearing the name of that route, for ease of identification by passengers.

In 1876 and 1878 trials were carried out with steam tram engines. It was thought that additional profits could be generated for the tramway company by eliminating the need for horses. A number of other tramways across the country also experimented with steam traction, but concerns were expressed that these vehicles would frighten horses and could be dangerous. In areas where they were used, stringent regulations were applied requiring the engines to consume their own smoke and for the "motion" to be completely covered as near to the road surface as possible. Steam tram engines found no favour with Sheffield Corporation and the idea was not pursued any further.

In July 1896 Sheffield Corporation took over the running of the city's tram network, becoming one of the first local councils to be authorised to operate tramways itself. A committee was then formed to look at the more technologically advanced forms of traction then in use on other tramways in Britain and abroad, which recommended the use of electrical propulsion using an overhead current collection system. At this time there was no national electricity supply available and very few existing local suppliers were capable of providing the amount of electric current needed for expanding electric tramways. Because of this, in many cases the only solution was for tramway

Above: For a short period in 1952–53 some Sheffield trams and buses carried an experimental green livery, but following widespread disapproval from the general public this soon reverted to the standard blue and cream colours. 11 trams were painted all-over green and 12 trams received a two-tone green colour scheme. Here Standard car 216 stands in Weedon Street, near Tinsley depot, in the all-over green livery on 4 August 1952. **Howard Turner**

Left: In this May 1955 view of Fitzalan Square looking towards the site of the old Castle Market, Sheffield Corporation-built Standard car 64 is seen on the right nearest the camera bound for Darnall with an unidentified car behind it and, on the left, Cravens-built car 452 on a service for Wadsley Bridge crossing over High Street and Commercial Street where the present day tramway runs. Note the imposing statue of King Edward VII, which is still standing today, and the substantial tram shelter.
Howard Turner

operators to generate their own electricity. A power station was built for the Sheffield Corporation Tramways Department on Kelham Island by the River Don between Alma Street and Mowbray Street, which is now used as Kelham Island Industrial Museum. Feeder cables from here supplied power to the extremities of the network, eventually covering over 40 miles of route. The first electric services to Nether Edge and Tinsley started operating on 5 September 1899, followed by the Walkley route on 18 September and Pitsmoor on 27 September. November 1902 saw the withdrawal of the last horse trams from the Hillsborough route.

Rotherham Corporation's tram route to Tinsley was connected to the Sheffield tram network in 1905 and through running between the two systems began. However, ill feeling between the two operators came to the surface from time to time, leading to the withdrawal of through services from September 1914 to May 1915 during which time passengers had to change trams at Tinsley or use the competing railway services.

The early years of the 20th century saw further expansion of the Sheffield network, with new routes opening to Intake in 1902, Middlewood in 1913, Millhouses in 1926 and Meadowhead in 1928 to name but a few. 1934 saw the opening of the last extension to Lane Top via Firth Park, but meanwhile the Petre Street route closed in 1925 followed by Nether Edge in 1934 and Fulwood via Fulwood Road in 1936. During World War I Sheffield purchased 20 second-hand double-deck trams from London because of wartime shortages and to replace a number of single-deck vehicles, some of which were sold to other operators. Damage to the tram fleet (and tramway infrastructure) by air raids during World War II led Sheffield Corporation to purchase 24 further second-hand trams, this time from Bradford and Newcastle. In 1946 the corporation built a new streamlined tramcar numbered 501 and known as a "Jubilee" car because 1946 was the 50th anniversary of the takeover of the city's tramways by the corporation. This was the prototype for a fleet of 35

Right: Brush car 433 of 1920 rounds the curve from Leopold Street to Fargate en route to Sheffield Lane Top in June 1955. The large Wilson Peck building still stands.
Howard Turner

Left: From left to right, rail grinder 330 (now preserved at Crich) and Standard cars 86 and 32 are seen stabled in Tenter Street depot in the city centre on 3 February 1957. Car 330 was one of ten trams purchased from Bradford Corporation in 1943, and had its top deck removed when it was converted to a works vehicle in 1951. This view shows the two variants of Sheffield Corporation livery, with car 86 carrying the early 1900s version and 32 the later version used on trams and buses from the 1930s onwards. **Howard Turner**

Right: Standard car 296 is seen at Millhouses in September 1960 about to reverse onto the crossover for its journey back to Vulcan Road. Standard cars dating from 1936 onwards were built to a modified design and were commonly known as "domed roof" cars. Behind it are sister vehicle 281 on the left and Roberts car 507 on the right. To the left is the former Millhouses loop line, which had closed at the end of August, shortly before this photo was taken. **Howard Turner**

more trams of this design, built by Charles Roberts & Co in Wakefield between 1950 and 1952, but even before the last of these had been delivered the city council decided in 1951 to abandon the tram network and replace it with buses. Fulwood–Malin Bridge was the first route to be converted to bus operation in January 1952, and a petition was circulated among the residents and traders in an unsuccessful bid to get their tram route reinstated. The next route to close was Ecclesall–Middlewood in March 1954, and from 1956 onwards two route closures per year were achieved until the last route between Beauchief and Vulcan Road, Tinsley, closed on 8 October 1960. An illuminated car, followed by a procession of 14 trams carrying specially booked passengers and guests of the city council, set out from Tenter Street depot on that very wet evening for a final run to Beauchief and back to the city centre. Dignitaries and their honoured guests, having ridden on streamlined car 510, the decorated official last tram, then headed to the Town Hall for a ceremony to mark the occasion, while those privileged to hold appropriate tickets rode on cars bound for Tinsley Depot or Queens Road Works. Trams headed for the latter point were some of those destined for preservation.

Left: Roberts car 506 passes the Midland Bank (now the Banker's Draft pub) at the site of the present day Castle Square tram stop with a service to Vulcan Road, Tinsley in 1960. Since this photo was taken, the infamous "hole in the road" has been and gone. Note the rear platform bus on the left, and the typical motor cars of the period. **Tom Robinson**

FORMER SHEFFIELD TRAMS IN
PRESERVATION

The Tramway Museum Society was formed in 1955 with the aim of preserving a representative sample of trams from across Britain plus a few from overseas. In 1959 the TMS acquired the museum site at Crich, Derbyshire, on part of the trackbed of a mineral railway built by George Stephenson to link Crich quarry with Ambergate. Crich is located just 25 miles from Sheffield. Until this time no museum devoted to tramcar history and preservation had existed anywhere in the country, although there were small groups that had taken possession of tramcars and associated equipment from tramway operators which they had then stored in temporary locations in the hope that a permanent home could be found for them at some unspecified date in the future at a site yet to be identified.

Crich was initially intended as a temporary home for just one Sheffield tram, but in the event a total of seven of the city's fleet were saved for preservation at Crich (including Britain's oldest operational tram, horse car 15) and three elsewhere: one at the Living Museum of the North at Beamish, County Durham, one at the East Anglia Transport Museum, Lowestoft, and one at the South Yorkshire Transport Museum in Aldwarke, Rotherham.

Left: Newcastle car 114 at the Town stop at Beamish on 4 March 2017. Built by Hurst Nelson & Co in Motherwell in 1901, this tram was one of many sold to Sheffield in 1941 to replace war-damaged vehicles. **Paul Abell**

Right: Car 264, built by United Electric Car Company in Preston in 1907 (not to be confused with Standard car 264 at Crich) is preserved at Beamish, where it is seen approaching the Beamish Entrance stop having just climbed the hill from the Pockerley waggonway on 8 April 2017. **Paul Abell**

Above: Standard car 189 on display in the depot at Crich on 21 September 2019. Behind it is Johannesburg car 60, built by United Electric Car Company in Preston (as with 15 of the Sheffield cars of 1907 vintage) and exported to South Africa. **Alan Yearsley**

Right: Standard car 264 on show in the exhibition hall at Crich on 7 November 2015 as part of a "timeline" display of trams through the ages. **Robert Pritchard**

TABLE I: PRESERVED SHEFFIELD TRAMS

Number	Type	Built by	Status	Notes
Crich Tramway Village				
15	Single-deck horse tram	Starbuck of Birkenhead, 1874	Operational (normally on static display)	Carries Brightside red and cream livery. Britain's oldest operational tram.
46	Single-deck electric tram	G.F. Milnes, 1899	Stored off-site	Usually ran on the Walkley route.
74	Double-deck electric tram	Electric Railway, Tramway and Carriage Works, Preston, 1900	Operational	Has a short top cover of distinctive design. Sold to Gateshead 1922.
189	Double-deck electric tram	Sheffield Corporation Transport Department, 1934	Static exhibit	
264	Double-deck electric tram	Sheffield Corporation Transport Department, 1937	Static exhibit	
330	Single-deck electric tram (non-passenger)	English Electric, 1919	Operational	Second-hand from Bradford, originally double-deck, converted to single-deck rail grinder 1951.
510	Double-deck electric tram	Charles Roberts & Co, Horbury, Wakefield, 1950	Operational	Sheffield's official last (first generation) tram. Carries "Sheffield's last tram" decals.
Beamish, the Living Museum of the North				
264	Double-deck electric tram	United Electric Car Company, Preston, 1907	Operational	Rebuilt with fully enclosed upper deck 1926. Now restored to original condition with open balcony ends. This is car 264 from the old numbering series, not to be confused with 264 at Crich.
East Anglia Transport Museum, Lowestoft				
513	Double-deck electric tram	Charles Roberts & Co, Horbury, Wakefield, 1950	Operational	On long-term loan from Beamish.
South Yorkshire Transport Museum				
460	Double-deck electric tram	Cravens, Sheffield, 1926	Static exhibit	Only the lower deck remains.

Left: Car 74 was built as an open top tram by the Electric Railway & Carriage Company (which later became the United Electric Car Company) in Preston in 1900, and had a short top cover added in 1909. It was sold to Gateshead in 1922 and withdrawn in 1951, after which the lower deck was sold and converted to a garden shed. In the early 1990s it was restored to operational condition and has run at Crich since 1995. Here is it seen at the halfway point at Wakebridge on 1 April 2012. **Paul Abell**

Below: Roberts car 510 was Sheffield's official last tram in 1960, at least until the launch of Supertram in 1994, and has resided at the National Tramway Museum at Crich since shortly after the closure of the city's first generation tram network. Here it is seen passing the entrance to the depot fan as it approaches the Town End terminus on 7 November 2015. Just visible at the top of the photo is Crich war memorial tower, known locally as Crich Stand. **Robert Pritchard**

Horse car 15, Britain's oldest operational tram, carries the Brightside route red and cream colour scheme. Here the horse is seen being attached to the tram as it prepares to depart from the Town End terminus at Crich on 17 May 2014. **Paul Abell**

THE SUPERTRAM PROJECT

L ittle more than a decade after the closure of the original Sheffield tram system consideration was already being given to the construction of a modern equivalent as part of the Sheffield/ Rotherham Land Use Transportation Study (S/RLUTS), which looked at likely requirements for passenger transportation into the 1990s. In order to address an anticipated growth in the service industries and an increase in demand for travelling into the city centre, the four-year study examined various different transport options, including a streetcar system serving the main routes in and out of the Sheffield city centre and also an extension to Rotherham. Its final report, published in 1976, recommended the safeguarding of alignments on radial corridors to Stannington, Middlewood, Shiregreen, Rotherham, Mosborough, Jordanthorpe and Totley for the eventual construction of a "Segregated Passenger Transport System" (SPTS) such as a modern tramway.

In 1974, whilst the study was ongoing, the South Yorkshire Passenger Transport Executive (SYPTE) was created through a reorganisation of local Government. Having taken over the bus fleets of Sheffield, Rotherham and Doncaster Corporations to become almost the sole bus operator in South Yorkshire, under the terms of the Transport Act 1968 the newly created PTE was also tasked with planning and developing an integrated public transport system for the county. The PTE could have also assumed responsibility for local rail services; however, its Director General at the time said that he saw no future for the railways in South Yorkshire.

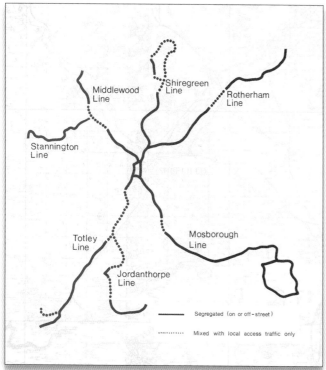

Above: A map of the seven alignments that the Sheffield/Rotherham Land Use Transportation Study recommended be safeguarded for the eventual construction of a "Segregated Passenger Transport System". **Courtesy SYPTE**

Above: One of the proposals considered under the Sheffield/Rotherham Land Use Transportation Study was a driverless "minitram" system, which would have connected the Sheffield station with Moorfoot. Despite its name this was not a tram system at all – rather than running on-street, the vehicles would have run on special guideways, most of which would have been overhead. The idea was abandoned as the study team did not consider it to represent good value for money and the Sheffield public thought it environmentally obtrusive. This artist's impression shows how the system would have looked crossing the "Hole in the Road" at Castle Square. **Courtesy Robert Matthew, Johnson-Marshall & Partners**

In publishing its Transport Development Plan in 1978, the PTE made a number of references to light rail in its medium- to long-term proposals and commented that "electric traction is the most likely future alternative for all longer-term transit systems in the county". The document concluded: "A segregated transit system could have notable advantages in reliability, cleanliness, quietness, higher acceleration and average speeds and cheapness of operation." The high cost of establishing such a system was considered a major drawback, but the PTE approved the S/RLUTS findings regarding SPTS nonetheless.

Left: An early mock-up of a Supertram is seen outside Sheffield Cathedral on 12 September 1987. It would remain here for a fortnight and was used to house an exhibition staged as part of an intense period of public consultation on the stalled project. Behind the wooden mock up is Sheffield Corporation Tramways No. 15, a single-deck horse tram, which is preserved at Crich Tramway Village. This was also part of the exhibition and allowed visitors to see just how much trams elsewhere in the world had improved. **Paul Jackson**

Below: An Official Journal of the European Communities notice placed by SYPTE seeking expressions of interest in the operation and maintenance of the Supertram system. **Courtesy SYPTE**

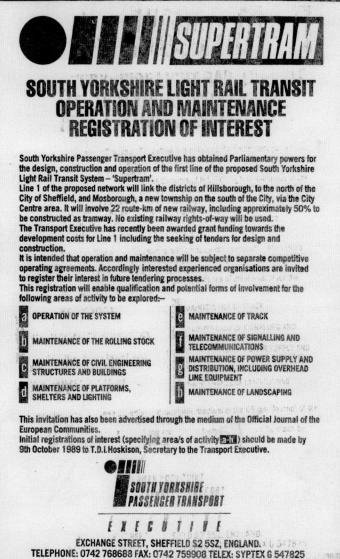

A similar approval in the County Structure Plan followed in 1979 and Sheffield City Council was thus asked as the planning authority to protect the alignments from other future developments. The 1980 report, The Future Development of Public Transport in Sheffield – Results of Preliminary Investigation, then proposed a feasibility study to ascertain how best to improve public transport in the city.

The SPTS Working Group, which was led by the PTE and formed of staff from County Engineering and Planning departments, reassessed transport demands in the seven radial corridors and subsequently decided to concentrate efforts on the routes to Hillsborough, in the north-west of the city, and the developing area of Mosborough, in south-east Sheffield, to determine the most cost-effective transport system. It reviewed in great detail the options available, including bus-based systems such as trolleybuses and guided busways, and also various on-street and segregated (overhead/ground level/underground) rail systems.

A "minitram" system with small, driverless electric vehicles had at one time been considered, but the idea was thrown out as the Sheffield public did not like the largely elevated system and the study team did not consider it to represent good value for money. A similar scheme in the USA suffered a cost overrun of 800%.

With speed being restricted by frequent stops, steep gradients and a lack of complete segregation, vehicle size and accessibility were then considered in order to determine the preferred solution. The PTE's pioneering use of articulated buses in Britain had led to some savings in productivity, and high capacity vehicles such as these could be given priority at traffic light controlled junctions; however, without complete segregation such vehicles would be limited to 18 m in length. A light rail system with grooved rails providing positive on-street guidance would allow trams of up to a maximum length of around 60 m to be legally operated, thus offering much greater savings in productivity.

In terms of accessibility, many of Sheffield's bus routes at the time terminated in the city's Central Bus Station, which was situated in the bottom of the Sheaf Valley alongside the railway station. Faced with a steep climb from here, many passengers then used the "City Clipper" buses to reach the city centre. This, it was said, indicated a demand for a public transport system providing greater accessibility into

the city, and although trams would only use the same streets as buses (the City Council did not want public transport reintroduced in pedestrianised areas such as Fargate), a light rail system would be able to transport people directly into the city centre. Trams would also offer significant environmental benefits over buses. Greater accessibility in the suburbs would be provided through frequent stops, with local bus services offering connections into housing estates and retail areas.

A 1983 report to South Yorkshire County Council recommended a modern tramway system as the preferred option. If segregation and thus journey time reductions and increased reliability could be achieved, a light rail system would be most cost effective. A trolleybus system could not be justified as the limitations on vehicle size would mean that such a system could not produce the productivity sufficient to finance the investment. Cost comparisons did, however, indicate that trolleybuses could offer savings in operating costs if they were used to replace diesel buses.

PARLIAMENTARY POWERS

The South Yorkshire Light Transit Bill was deposited in Parliament on 19 November 1985, seeking powers for the PTE to develop and operate a light rail system, to authorise the construction of works and the acquisition of land for the purpose. As proposed the line would have started at Winn Gardens, Middlewood and run towards the city centre via Langsett Road, Infirmary Road, Netherthorpe Road, Glossop Road, West Street, Church Street and High Street, before continuing along Commercial Street, over Park Square, past the railway station and then up through the Norfolk Park Estate and Gleadless to Birley and Halfway. A branch from Stannington would have joined the main route at Hillsborough Corner, whilst a second branch would have run from Gleadless Townend to Herdings Park; but before the Bill reached the Opposed Bills Committee in the House of Commons, at the request of Sheffield City Council, the PTE withdrew the line from Malin Bridge to Stannington.

There were two official objectors to the scheme, National Car Parks Ltd (NCP) and a residents' group; however, doubts over Sheffield City Council's commitment towards the project also caused delays. SCC had only recently become involved following the passing of the Local Government Act 1985 and the abolition of South Yorkshire County Council, upon which it became responsible for all highway matters for non-trunk roads. The deregulation of the bus industry in October 1986 caused it to question the viability of the project. The original concept was for an integrated public transport system, which would have maximised revenue and minimised costs. Supertram, as it had become known, would have largely replaced buses along the

aforementioned routes; however, with the PTE no longer able to direct bus operation in the area, Supertram would instead have to compete for the market share.

In order for SCC to give its full backing to the Bill, which had twice been stalled in the Commons, the economic case for the proposed system was reassessed and an intensive period of consultation took place in September 1987. A public exhibition was held on the Cathedral forecourt during the period 12–26 September, housed in a wooden mock-up of a Supertram. 65% of visitors said that they wanted the scheme to go ahead: 67% of those interviewed in their homes said likewise. Public meetings were also arranged in various areas affected by the proposals, but these only attracted a fairly low turnout and most of the comments received were negative. Subsequent analysis indicated that this, however, was mainly due to a lack of knowledge of the proposals.

Encouraged by the positive public response and its reassessment of the project, which concluded that there was still an economic case for Supertram, at its October 1987 meeting SCC gave the scheme

Below: The original Line 1 route would have seen trams running through the Manor Estate via a widened Wulfric Road. This plan would have involved many of the houses either side of the road being replaced, but following extensive public consultation Sheffield City Council instead decided that it would renovate the properties rather than rebuild them. The PTE was thus asked to plan a new tram route running from Manor Top straight down City Road. **Courtesy SYPTE**

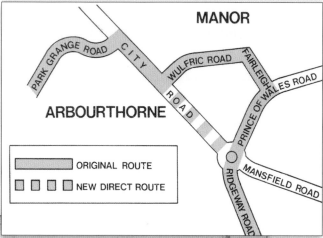

Below: An artist's impression of a Supertram running along the new route along City Road in a clearway. **Courtesy SYPTE**

Above: To update businesses and residents of progress with the Line 2 route to Meadowhall, SYPTE published a series of factsheets entitled "Supertram in the Lower Don Valley (Line 2)". Factsheet 5, issued late in 1988, contained this artist's impression of a Supertram travelling into the city centre on the viaduct alongside the Sheffield Parkway. **Courtesy SYPTE**

its unreserved backing and thus released the Bill in Parliament. The Bill finally passed the Commons Stage on 20 April 1988. Objections from a group of residents and traders, and some also from the City of Sheffield & District Chamber of Trade, were later presented to the House of Lords Opposed Committee; however, on 27 October 1988, nearly three years after its deposition, the Bill received Royal Assent.

THE DON VALLEY LINE

Various conditions were attached to SCC's approval of the Middlewood–Halfway Line 1 route; principally an alteration to the alignment of the line between Park Grange Road and Manor Top, to enable the council to renovate parts of the Manor Estate rather than rebuild it, and the provision of a line to serve the Lower Don Valley, Line 2. The aim of the latter was to aid with the regeneration of this former industrial area after the collapse of the city's steel industry. It would also serve the various stadia then being built for the 1991 World Student Games. SCC further requested that if the second Bill was passed in Parliament, the depot, which was originally to have been sited at Halfway, should instead be built in the Don Valley, and construction of the system should be rephased so that the Meadowhall line would be opened first. It was at this point envisaged that it would be operational in time for the 1991 events.

On 24 February 1988 the South Yorkshire Passenger Transport Authority (PTA) authorised the PTE to undertake a study to identify the route of this second line. Amongst various other considerations, the proposed line had to connect with that from Middlewood to Halfway to form

a network and, in line with earlier proposals, it would also have to be capable of extension to Rotherham. The proposed Sheffield City Airport similarly had to be taken into account and had this been successful a further extension may have been necessary.

Three potential routes were outlined in the study:

- Route A, running along the general line of Brightside Lane and Meadow Hall Road;
- Route B, broadly following Attercliffe Road and Attercliffe Common; and
- Route C, running along, or next to, the railway line in the Woodbourn Road area, under Staniforth Road and Coleridge Road and then following the line of the Sheffield & Tinsley Canal through Attercliffe Hill Top and Carbrook.

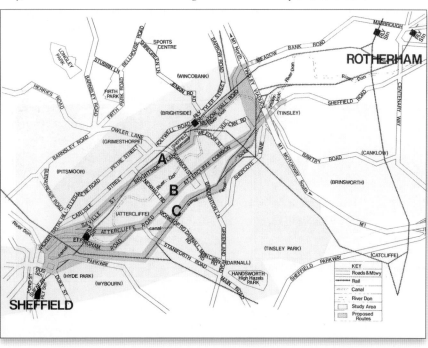

Right: The three potential routes, which were outlined as part of the SYPTE's study into the Meadowhall Line 2 route. **Courtesy SYPTE**

The study team, which was led by The MVA Consultancy, later recommended that the Brightside Lane route was not suitable, but Routes B and C both fulfilled the purpose of serving the East End Park area of Attercliffe and the planned shopping and leisure development at Meadowhall.

Following the completion of the aforementioned study in July 1988 a Bill was presented to Parliament that November. This sought powers for the construction of an almost completely segregated route, leaving the original line via a delta junction at Park Square and then heading over a new viaduct on the south side of the Sheffield Parkway to Bernard Road. It would then run parallel to a widened Cricket Inn Road in a cutting, cross the Sheffield Parkway on a bridge, and run alongside the new depot site at Nunnery. Continuing north-eastwards it would cross over the former Manchester, Sheffield & Lincolnshire Railway and then follow Woodbourn Road to the junction with Staniforth Road, cross the Sheffield & South Yorkshire Canal and run along its north side to eventually join the railway route towards Tinsley, leaving this just before the M1 viaduct to take the alignment of the former Smithywood line across the River Don and terminate next to the main railway line from Sheffield at Meadowhall.

This second Bill was unopposed in Parliament and in fact received support from many quarters including the Chamber of Trade, which had previously objected to the route through the city centre. Prior to the final reading of the Bill, however, a furious row developed in Parliament with two opposition MPs threatening to delay all Parliamentary business unless another Private Bill appertaining to facilities for coal imports was either dropped or amended. Common sense, fortunately, prevailed and the Bill finally received Royal Assent on 21 December 1989.

South Yorkshire Supertram Ltd, a wholly owned subsidiary of the PTE and subsequently renamed South Yorkshire Light Rail Ltd, was created in 1989 to take the project forward.

FUNDING

Towards the end of 1988 an application was made to Government for an infrastructure grant, under Section 56 of the Transport Act 1968, to finance the construction of Line 1. The same approach was used for all public transport infrastructure schemes outside London and had been successful in obtaining funding for Manchester's Metrolink; however, whilst discussions were ongoing the criteria for the payment of such grants was radically altered. Traditionally social benefits had been used as the main justification for funding, but the new rules meant that benefits to users had to be accounted for through higher fares. The benefits that the scheme would bring to non-users (by alleviating traffic congestion, for example) was instead used as the rationale for the investment.

November 1989 brought a further setback to the scheme, with the Government informing local authorities that resources would not be available in 1990–91 for the building of the Meadowhall line, citing that many millions of pounds were already been invested in the Road Programme. Sheffield Development Corporation, however, succeeded in its application at this time for

a £14 million grant to ensure the building of a highway through the Lower Don Valley. Urgent talks with Whitehall officials followed in an effort to keep the project moving forward and despite the willingness of private investors to contribute, as was required under the modified Section 56 guidelines, a further refusal for grant funding came in February 1990. £3.5 million was, however, allocated for the purpose of safeguarding the project and eventually taking it forward.

Minister for Public Transport, Roger Freeman, announced on 11 December 1990 that resources had been made available to fund the majority of the project's capital costs, expected to total £240 million. In announcing this, the largest local scheme to be approved outside of London in almost 20 years, Mr Freeman assured local poll-tax payers that they would not be funding the system (this later turned out not to be the case). Further financial support was to be provided by the Meadowhall Centre, the City Council, Sheffield Development Corporation and also the European Regional Development Fund. Progress with the scheme was further delayed, however, due to a political argument over possible council charge-capping, which was not resolved until April 1991.

CONSTRUCTION

Rather than having an in-house team, as had been done in Manchester during the development of Metrolink, in 1989 SYPTE appointed Turner & Townsend as project manager. Reporting directly to the Chief Executive of South Yorkshire Supertram Ltd, John Davies, the firm was responsible for a team of consultant technical advisors, the infrastructure and rolling stock contractors, and various other suppliers.

SCC's consultant arm, Design and Building Services was employed to give advice on structural, civil and highway engineering matters such as the preliminary swept path alignment, integrating the light

TABLE 1: PHASES OF SUPERTRAM CONSTRUCTION (USING CURRENT STOP NAMES)

Phase	Area of works
Phase 1	Meadowhall–Commercial Street/Sheffield Station
Phase 2	Sheffield Station–Spring Lane
Phase 3	Commercial Street–Cathedral
Phase 4	Cathedral–Shalesmoor
Phase 5	Spring Lane–Gleadless Townend–Herdings
Phase 6	Gleadless Townend–Donetsk Way
Phase 7	Donetsk Way–Halfway
Phase 8	Shalesmoor–Middlewood/Malin Bridge

Right: Jack Meredith, Chairman of the South Yorkshire Passenger Transport Authority, addresses the assembled crowd at the cutting of the first sod ceremony at Park Square on 16 September 1991.
Paul Jackson

Above: Contractors work on the overhead line equipment at Spring Lane on 8 May 1994. **Paul Jackson**

Above: The ongoing construction of the trackbed in Church Street on 12 March 1994. **Paul Jackson**

Left: By autumn 1993 track laying had progressed as far as White Lane, as seen in this 2 November view taken nearby what was then the local Kwik Save supermarket. Previously a ballroom, The Azena, on 12 February 1963 this was the first venue in the city at which the Beatles played. **Paul Jackson**

ROAD CLOSED

ROAD AHEAD CLOSED

Parkway Viaduct under construction on 2 May 1992. **Paul Jackson**

Right: Construction of the Line 1 route caused considerable disruption to the users of Sheffield's roads. Signs such as this one pictured at Park Grange Road on 7 October 1992 were a familiar sight around the city in the early 1990s. **Paul Jackson**

Below: A panoramic view of work in progress at Park Square on 7 November 1992. **Paul Jackson**

Left: An unidentified Class 158 approaches Sheffield on 30 June 1992, passing what is now the site of Norfolk Park Viaduct. **Paul Jackson**

Right: The slip-form paver could not be used where pointwork was to be installed and instead shuttering had to be used to form the channels into which the rails would be laid, as seen here at Gleadless Townend on 21 August 1994. **Paul Jackson**

Left: A visit to City Road on 10 July 1993 finds the new formation awaiting the installation of the concrete trackbed. **Paul Jackson**

Above: The nearby flats afford an aerial view of work on the construction of Brook Hill underpass on 16 September 1993. **Paul Jackson**

Right: A variety of engineering vehicles were used on the system during its construction. Two such examples are found at the Granville Road stop on 18 June 1994. **Paul Jackson**

Left: A Mainline bus passes construction works at the junction of West Street and Carver Lane on 26 June 1993. **Paul Jackson**

CONSTRUCTION PHASES

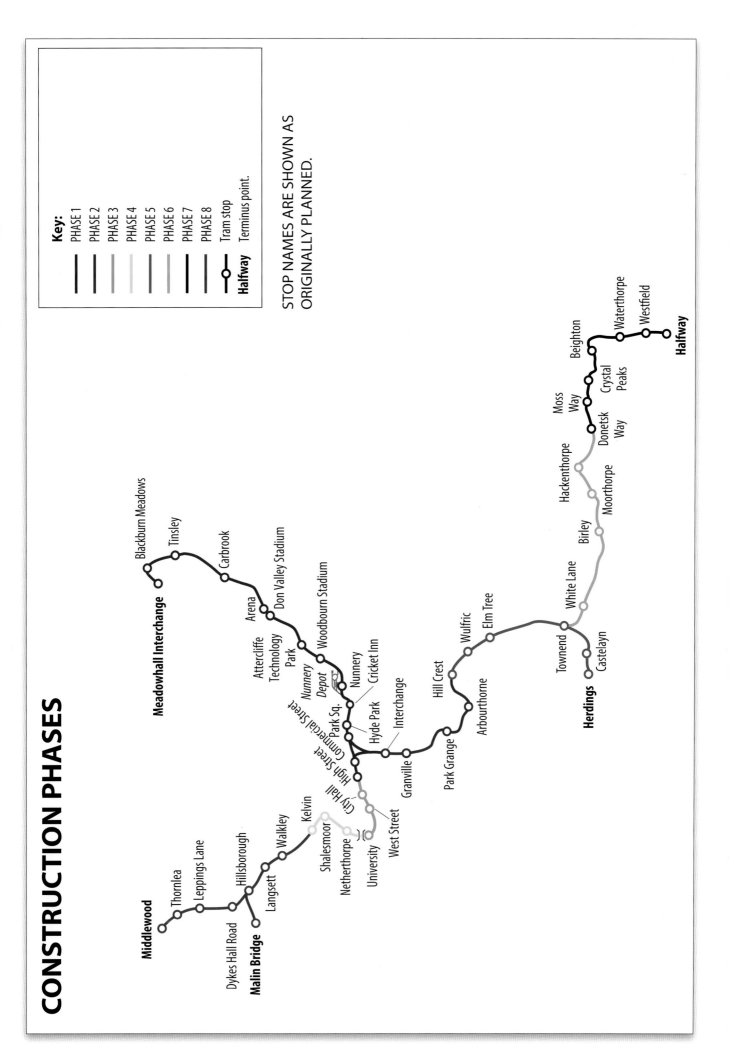

Key:
PHASE 1
PHASE 2
PHASE 3
PHASE 4
PHASE 5
PHASE 6
PHASE 7
PHASE 8
Halfway Tram stop
Terminus point.

STOP NAMES ARE SHOWN AS
ORIGINALLY PLANNED.

rail operation within the city's existing traffic control system and also the designs of major city centre viaducts and bridges. Kennedy & Donkin Transportation, which had earlier been involved in the Parliamentary promotion stage, acted as mechanical, electrical and railway engineering consultants. Public consultation and information matters were handled by Frank Graham Consulting Engineers. Race Cottam Associated, Globe Architects and Plan Design were consulted on matters concerning architecture and landscaping. Her Majesty's Railway Inspectorate and the police were also involved as and when required.

Following the offer of Government finance, the Passenger Transport Authority gave its approval for the scheme on 5 December 1990. After an exhaustive tendering process it was announced on the same date that Balfour Beatty Power Construction Ltd had been awarded the £73 million infrastructure contract and would be responsible for all civil and building work, including trackwork, power supply and distribution, signalling and the Nunnery depot. On 13 December 1990 Siemens plc was appointed to design, manufacture and commission the system's 25 trams. The companies later received contracts to provide core maintenance services, the responsibilities being split according to their areas of expertise.

Construction commenced on 5 August 1991, although the official cutting of the first sod took place a little over a month later in a ceremony at Park Square on 16 September. Carried out in phases, starting with the Meadowhall line as per the request of the City Council, the works would

then continue until 1995. The preceding map, which features the planned stop names – and a number of stops that were never built, shows the sequence of infrastructure works. This information is also given in Table 1, but for clarity the current stop names are used.

It is understood that the first phase of works, much of which used former railway alignments, were relatively straightforward, only requiring road closures at the six crossings (Bernard Road, Aston Street, Woodbourn Road, Staniforth Road, Shirland Lane and Alsing Road). The later phases, however, included a significant amount of on-street running and saw long periods of road closures and diversions.

Above: Marking a major milestone in the history of the Supertram system, 17 September 1993 saw the commencement of test running between Nunnery and Meadowhall. Here 1002, the first of the 25 Siemens-Duewag trams to be delivered to Sheffield, stands at Attercliffe with the pioneering gauging run. The first three trams underwent testing on Düsseldorf's Rheinischebahn system and were allocated four digit 1xxx numbers, which were applied to their cab fronts and lower bodysides. Other trams were briefly allocated numbers in this series, but they were only carried on card plaques inside the cabs; all trams were later renumbered into the more familiar 01–25 number range. **Paul Jackson**

Below: On 12 February 1994, a little over a month prior to the commencement of public operations, an unidentified tram stands at Fitzalan Square on a driver training run. **Paul Jackson**

Where possible, parts of the 22 km Middlewood–Halfway line were segregated either in central reservations, adjacent to the highway on verges or on undeveloped land. £2.5 million was allocated for landscaping works to ensure that the swept path of the tram would blend into the surrounding environment.

DRIVER TRAINING

Part of the Line 2 route was handed over to South Yorkshire Supertram in October 1993 to allow testing and driver training to take place. Driving training commenced the following month, whilst trial running started in the latter half of that December and in order to satisfy the Railway Inspectorate, Fitzalan Square–Meadowhall "ghost" services were operated between 06.00 and midnight for the four weeks from 24 January 1994.

Prior to the commencement of driver training six members of Supertram's senior staff, none of whom had any previous experience in the rail industry, made visits to Manchester Metrolink and the

National Tramway Museum at Crich (now Crich Tramway Village). These visits allowed them to gain an appreciation of light rail operations and also some practical experience. They were also given an intensive five-week course, two weeks of which were in driver training, at Hong Kong's Tuen Mun Light Rail Transit system.

Anybody applying for a tram driving position was required to be in possession of a valid motor vehicle licence and before going through the qualification process they were subject to nine weeks of training, including an average of 30 hours of practical training. The competence of trainee drivers was initially assessed by a senior staff member from the driver licensing authority of Düsseldorf's Rheinischebahn system, now simply Rheinbahn, which four senior members of Supertram staff had visited for several days prior to the delivery of the first tram to Sheffield in order to gain first-hand experience of driving one of the vehicles. Like the Sheffield system, the Rheinischebahn network includes both segregated and on-street running. A test driver from the Rheinischebahn also came over to Sheffield for a two-week period to advise on the commissioning of the trams.

Prior to the start of Phase 2 operations, four members of Supertram's training staff made visits to other British tram systems to gain experience in on-street driving. A two-day course at Blackpool was followed by five days of training in Manchester, after which they then had almost a week of independent driving between Fitzalan Square and Spring Lane before training their colleagues who were already familiar with driving on the Meadowhall route.

OPERATION

The system opened in stages as construction progressed, public services commencing with the 06.00 departure from Meadowhall on 21 March 1994. The first service, worked by tram 13, was unsurprisingly full and standing, and during the first weeks of operation the trams continued to be extremely busy with Sheffield residents and others from further afield taking a ride. Most seemed delighted with the smooth ride and spacious vehicles. Customer service staff were provided on board trams for a time to help familiarise passengers with the new system, and to also undertake revenue protection. Random ticket checks of approximately 25% of all

Below: Invited guests crowd onto the platform at Meadowhall on the morning of 21 March 1994 ahead of a press special to the city centre, which would be worked by car 01. On the right is car 13, which would work the inaugural public service, the 06.00 departure for Fitzalan Square. **Paul Jackson**

Right: Car 01 is pictured at Fitzalan Square on the morning of 21 March 1994 having worked a special service for press and invited guests from Meadowhall. It was followed into the city centre by the inaugural public service, the 06.00 departure from Meadowhall, worked by car 13. **Paul Jackson**

TABLE 2: COMMENCEMENT OF PUBLIC SERVICES

Date	Section
21 March 1994	Fitzalan Square–Meadowhall
22 August 1994	Fitzalan Square–Spring Lane
5 December 1994	Spring Lane–Gleadless Townend
18 February 1995	Fitzalan Square–Cathedral
27 February 1995	Cathedral–Shalesmoor
27 March 1995	Gleadless Townend–Halfway
3 April 1995	Gleadless Townend–Herdings
23 October 1995	Shalesmoor–Middlewood/Malin Bridge

Left: On 23 May 1994 HRH The Princess Royal, Princess Anne officially opens Supertram by unveiling a plaque at Park Square. This has since been relocated to Nunnery depot to avoid vandalism. Cllr Jack Meredith, Chairman of the South Yorkshire Passenger Transport Authority is seen on the left. **Richard Bolsover**

Below: On 12 June 1994 tram 12 approaches Fitzalan Square (wrong line) with a service from Meadowhall. Until the extension of services through to Cathedral in February 1995 all Meadowhall services used the inbound platform here, whilst those on the Line 1 route used the outbound platform. The two lines were effectively considered parallel single lines as far as Park Square. **Paul Jackson**

Below: Tram 02 heads down High Street on 18 February 1995, the first day of public services to/from Cathedral. At this point the coloured route system had yet to be introduced and trams carried temporary destination blinds in the lower windscreen. **Paul Jackson**

Left: Old meets new at Cathedral on 17 October 1995 as Sheffield Corporation Tramways horse tram 15, which used to operate on the Brightside route, is posed alongside Supertram 07. The horse tram is the only original Sheffield tram to have run on Supertram metals, between Vicar Lane and Cathedral. At the time it was being kept at Kelham Island Museum and was hired in to help publicise the imminent opening of the extension from Shalesmoor to Middlewood and Malin Bridge on 23 October. Marking the completion of the system, this was celebrated with three days of free travel across the network and unsurprisingly, especially as this coincided with the half-term holiday, trams were again full and standing. **Paul Jackson**

Right: 04 is pictured at Spring Lane on 1 July 1994. A temporary stop block prevents trams from proceeding any further towards City Road. **Paul Jackson**

passengers carried found that 3.5% did not have a validated ticket. A small number of passengers had no ticket at all!

Passenger numbers soon settled down, however, and outside of shop opening hours the trams were often lightly loaded. Although the trams were frequent, because of their route through the Lower Don Valley the end-to-end journey time was approximately 16 minutes and compared unfavourably with direct buses, which could get from the city centre to Meadowhall in as little as 12 minutes. One major problem was the excessive amount of time trams spent at each stop, up to 30 seconds in the early days, even when there was nobody boarding or alighting! Much of the delay was attributed to the drawn-out procedure to close the doors. Fortunately as drivers became more experienced the stopping time was reduced and nowadays trams only observe stops (except the termini!) by request (requesting stopping was introduced around 1999).

Following an official opening on 23 May 1994, with HRH The Princess Royal, Princess Anne travelling on a tram from Meadowhall to Park Square where she unveiled a commemorative plaque, on 22 August 1994 the second phase of the Supertram network, Fitzalan Square–Spring Lane, opened to the public. Services were extended to

Gleadless Townend from 5 December 1994, with an 8-minute daytime frequency then being in operation on both routes, this requiring five trams to provide the service on the Meadowhall line and eight on the Gleadless route.

In preparation for the opening of further extensions the night of 16–17 February 1995 saw the operation of a gauging run through Sheffield city centre. Services to Cathedral commenced on the following Saturday, 18 February 1995. Those from Meadowhall used the facing crossover on the approach to the stop to turn back in the inbound platform (inbound and outbound are relative to the Park Square delta junction), whilst those from Gleadless set down passengers and continued empty to Shalesmoor for driver training purposes. Passenger-carrying services to Shalesmoor started on 27 February.

A sixth tram was used on Meadowhall services from 25 February 1995 as experience had shown that the timetable could no longer be maintained with just five vehicles; however, a 9-minute service frequency was later introduced to obviate the need for this additional tram.

A coloured route system was introduced in September 1995, but with subsequent timetable changes several of these routes have since been lost to service changes. On 20 April 1996 tram 20 calls at Manor Top with a Green Route service from Cathedral to Herdings Park.
Paul Jackson

A gauging run to Halfway took place late on the evening of 5 March 1995 using tram 22. Public services over this part of the network started on 26 March 1995, with the operation of a free preview service between Halfway and Gleadless Townend. Normal services began the following day, whilst those to Herdings Park started on 3 April 1995, both operating through to Shalesmoor at 12-minute intervals during the day. The frequency of services to and from Herdings Park was quickly reduced, however, as passenger numbers failed to meet expectations. Faced with trams running almost empty between Herdings Park and Gleadless Townend, and the realisation that it would be impossible to operate the intended six-minute frequencies on the core routes (every 12 minutes at the extremities) once the network was fully open, a new timetable was introduced from the start of September 1995.

Coloured route system

With this new timetable a coloured route system was introduced and this has subsequently been used on all publicity and displayed on the tram destination indicators, with a coloured square to the left of the destination. Blue was initially used to indicate trams working between Halfway and Cathedral. Yellow represented trams on the Meadowhall–Shalesmoor route, and Herdings Park–Cathedral was at that time the Green Route. Sundays-only Halfway–Meadowhall and Herdings Park–Shalesmoor services were respectively represented by purple and orange.

With the opening of the lines to Middlewood and Malin Bridge the following month the Blue and Orange Routes were extended through to Malin Bridge and the Yellow Route to Middlewood. At this time services operated between 06.00 and midnight on weekdays, with trams running every 10 minutes on the Blue and Yellow Routes during the day, giving a service every five minutes through the city centre. Two trams per hour were provided on the Green Route, a total of 22 trams being required to fulfil the timetable. 21 trams were required in the off-peak.

Privatisation

Although much of the project was funded through public grants, in giving its approval to the scheme the Government stipulated that the operation and maintenance of the system should be the responsibility

TABLE 3: ESTIMATED PASSENGER JOURNEYS MADE ON SUPERTRAM PER FINANCIAL YEAR

Year	Passenger journeys (millions)
1994–1995	2.2
1995–1996	5.3
1996–1997	7.8
1997–1998	9.2
1998–1999	10.4
1999–2000	10.9
2000–2001	11.1
2001–2002	11.4
2002–2003	11.5
2003–2004	12.3
2004–2005	12.8
2005–2006	13.1
2006–2007	14.0
2007–2008	14.8
2008–2009	15.0
2009–2010	14.7
2010–2011	15.0
2011–2012	15.0
2012–2013	14.4
2013–2014	12.6
2014–2015	11.5
2015–2016	11.6
2016–2017	12.6
2017–2018	12.3
2018–2019	11.9

Above: Since the introduction of the coloured route system, services between Meadowhall and Middlewood have always been referred to as the Yellow Route. On 12 August 2018 Pretty Little Thing-liveried 118 approaches Fitzalan Square/Ponds Forge with a service to Middlewood. **Ian Beardsley**

TABLE 4: OFF-PEAK MONDAY–SATURDAY TRAM SERVICES FROM SEPTEMBER 1995

Route Colour	Service	Interval	Trams Required
Yellow	Middlewood–Meadowhall	10 minutes	8
Blue	Malin Bridge–Halfway	10 minutes	12[1]
Green	Cathedral–Herdings Park	30 minutes	2

Note: [1] Later reduced to 11.

TABLE 5: SUNDAY TRAM SERVICES FROM SEPTEMBER 1995

Route Colour	Service	Interval	Trams Required
Yellow	Middlewood–Meadowhall	15 minutes	7[1]
Purple	Halfway–Meadowhall	15 minutes	5
Orange	Malin Bridge–Herdings Park	15 minutes	6[2]

Notes: [1] Later reduced to 6.
[2] Later reduced to 5.

Right: As the shops in Sheffield city centre did not open on Sundays, whereas those in Meadowhall did, the September 1995 timetable change saw the introduction of a Sundays-only direct service between Halfway and Meadowhall. Known as the Purple Route, this provided the first regular passenger service over the east curve at Park Square. Hitherto the only passenger services to use this had been specials running in connection with events at Sheffield Arena or Don Valley Stadium. En route to Meadowhall, 03 is pictured on the curve at Park Square on 25 October 1995. **Paul Jackson**

of the private sector. With this in mind South Yorkshire Supertram (No. 2) Ltd was set up in August 1991. Prior to it being sold off the company would first have to demonstrate that it could operate at a profit.

Annual ridership, which was expected to reach 22 million by the turn of the century, fell far short of predictions, however, with services outside of the peaks largely running empty in the early years. At the time this was variously blamed on competition from local bus operators, delays due to traffic congestion, complex ticketing and also poor marketing. The system was consequently operating at a loss, not only making any prospects of a sale look bleak, but also meaning that the borrowing that helped fund its construction could not be repaid, leaving local councils with over £80 million of debt. In an attempt to recoup its costs, in 1996 SYPTE advertised the system for sale, lock stock and barrel, including the assets (the infrastructure and rolling stock) which were originally intended to remain under the control of the PTE. It was thought this would gain interest from potential operators and rolling stock leasing companies, but in the end it was only the operation that was sold, South Yorkshire Supertram (No. 2) Ltd being transferred to Stagecoach on 20 December 1997 for £1.15 million. With this sale Stagecoach gained the concession to operate Supertram services until 31 March 2024.

Passenger numbers (Table 3) have climbed significantly under Stagecoach, the number of passenger journeys rising from 7.8 million in 1996–97 to a peak of 15 million in 2008–09. This figure was again reached in 2010–11 and 2011–12, but the number of passenger journeys has since fallen, largely as a result of the disruption caused by rail replacement works.

Timetable changes

With the Stagecoach takeover the timetable and indeed the coloured route system underwent something of an overhaul. The Sundays-only Purple and Orange Route services were lost and since then Sunday services have mirrored the usual weekday provision, albeit at a reduced frequency in most cases (until December 2019 Herdings Park services operated at a 20-minute frequency on Sundays instead of every 30 minutes in the week).

The Herdings Park–Cathedral Green Route was discontinued from 17 February 1997. Purple was then used to represent the new Herdings Park–Meadowhall services, which were initially routed round the east curve at Park Square, but were later rerouted via the city centre and reversed at Cathedral.

The various timetables then remained largely the same for many years, but on 23 October 2017 plans for a revised timetable were announced, with Supertram saying that which was then in place was "no longer fit for purpose". Traffic on Sheffield's roads had increased considerably and consequently it was becoming increasingly difficult

for services to maintain timings. The tight schedule meant that once delayed it was difficult for trams to make up any time and services sometimes had to be turned back short of their destination in order for trams to regain their booked workings back across the city.

Developed in partnership with SYPTE and implemented from 28 January 2018, the new timetable sought to address the various issues by allowing extra running time and longer turnarounds at the termini. Blue Route services were given an additional four to five minutes between Malin Bridge and Halfway, giving end-to-end

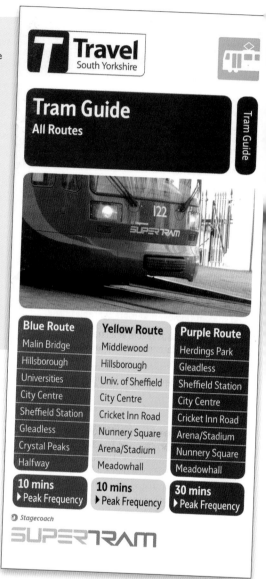

A 2010 copy of the Travel South Yorkshire Tram Guide, which provided information on how to use the tram network, including timetables for the three routes in operation at the time, a network map and a destination finder for arts, shopping and sports facilities in the city. **Courtesy SYPTE**

TABLE 6: BLUE ROUTE SERVICES STARTING/TERMINATING AT CRICKET INN ROAD, MONDAYS–FRIDAYS

To/from Malin Bridge														
Cricket Inn Road	05.24	05.44	06.04	06.53	07.13	16.06			Malin Bridge	09.09	19.27	19.51	23.35	23.55
Cathedral	05.30	05.50	06.10	06.59	07.19	16.12			Cathedral	09.28	19.44	20.08	23.52	00.12
Malin Bridge	05.47	06.07	06.27	07.17	07.37	16.30			Cricket Inn Road	09.34	19.50	20.14	23.58	00.18
To/from Halfway														
Cricket Inn Road	05.10	05.30	05.50	06.19	06.39	06.57	07.09	15.40	Halfway	09.23	18.55	19.27	19.47	23.17	23.37	23.57	00.17
Cathedral	-	-	-	-	-	-	07.17	-	Sheffield Station / Sheffield Hallam University	09.56	19.27	19.59	20.20	23.46	00.06	00.29	00.49
Sheffield Station / Sheffield Hallam University	05.15	05.35	05.55	06.24	06.44	07.02	07.22	15.45	Cathedral	10.01	19.34	20.06	20.31	23.56	00.16	-	-
Halfway	05.47	06.07	06.27	06.57	07.17	07.35	07.55	16.18	Cricket Inn Road	10.09	19.40	20.12	20.36	00.02	00.22	00.34	00.54

Note: Most intermediate times are not included.

journey times of a little under an hour. Yellow Route services were given an additional four minutes running time, Meadowhall–Middlewood then being timetabled to take approximately 40 minutes (journeys times in the off-peak and at weekends are shorter). Purple Route services were allowed an extra two minutes between Herdings Park and Cathedral, giving these a running time of 23 minutes.

The service frequency on the Blue and Yellow Routes was reduced from every ten to every 12 minutes during the off-peak period, a benefit of this being that it facilitated the introduction of tram-train services without the need for another major shake-up. The Sundays-only Purple Route services to Meadowhall were, however, lost with the introduction of tram-trains later in the year.

A further alteration to the Purple Route timetable came in December 2019, this seeing the unnecessary 20-minute frequency on Sundays and on Monday–Saturday evenings on this relatively lightly-used route reduced to half-hourly. Times of the first and last services were also amended – the last tram on Mondays–Saturdays being approximately 20 minutes later than under the January 2018 timetable, whilst on Sundays the first tram was timetabled to depart from Cricket Inn Road almost quarter of an hour earlier, and the last tram was six minutes earlier than before.

Early morning/late night services

At the time of writing the first services on a weekday morning start at approximately 05.30 and the last trams return towards the city centre at around midnight. These early morning and late night workings provide the rare sight of Blue and Purple Route services on the Meadowhall line as they enter service and later return to the depot; some also offer the opportunity to travel over the "rare" side of the delta junction as they travel directly to/from Halfway and Herdings Park (see Tables 6 and 7).

As with most other forms of public transport, Supertram runs to a revised timetable over the Christmas and New Year period (from 24 December to 1 January). This generally involves reduced service frequencies, early finishes on Christmas and New Year's Eve (the last trams running between 18.00 and 19.00) and no services on Christmas Day. Boxing Day sees the suspension of the Purple Route, whilst Blue Route services are diverted to Meadowhall via the city centre; the Yellow Route operates as usual. There are no trams to either Malin Bridge or Herdings Park on 26 December or 1 January. New Year's Day likewise sees an amended service on the Blue Route with trams from Halfway terminating in the city centre.

On most other Bank Holidays, a Sunday service is operated. Good Friday, however, sees a Saturday timetable in operation.

In some years additional services have been operated to and from Middlewood over the Christmas period in connection with football matches at Sheffield Wednesday's Hillsborough stadium.

TABLE 7: PURPLE ROUTE SERVICES STARTING/ TERMINATING AT CRICKET INN ROAD, MONDAYS–FRIDAYS

To/from Herdings Park					
Cricket Inn Road	05.25	05.55	Herdings Park	23.38	00.08
Cathedral	-	-	Sheffield Station / Sheffield Hallam University	23.56	00.26
Sheffield Station / Sheffield Hallam University	05.30	06.00	Cathedral	00.03	-
Herdings Park	05.48	06.18	Cricket Inn Road	00.09	00.31

Note: Most intermediate times are not included.

Above: Tram services operate from early morning until late evening, making it easy for people to get around the city at almost all hours of the day. On 30 January 2017 113 awaits departure from Halfway with a late evening service to Malin Bridge. Behind it is tram-train 399 204, which had failed whilst on test earlier that day. **Ian Beardsley**

THE ROUTES
DESCRIBED

Visitors to Sheffield will most likely have their first encounter with Supertram in the city centre, perhaps using the system to travel from either the railway station or bus interchange to one of the various sporting or concert venues in the city. Here we describe the three main routes out of the city (the tram-train route beyond Meadowhall South/Tinsley is detailed towards the end of this publication). All directions are given assuming that the reader is sitting in the direction of travel.

THE HALFWAY/HERDINGS LINE

As the current terminus of the Purple Route services from Herdings Park and tram-trains from Rotherham Parkgate, it could be said that Cathedral is the main tram stop in the city centre, and it therefore seems as good a place as any to start our journey. Like the majority of Supertram stops, Cathedral consists of two platforms. Trams towards Halfway, Herdings and Meadowhall, and tram-trains towards Parkgate, use the platform nearest the Cathedral Church of St Peter & St Paul, from which the stop takes its name. Those trams which reverse here cross to the inbound line using a facing crossover to the east of the stop. We board a Blue Route tram bound for Halfway and travel eastwards, following one of Sheffield Corporation Tramways' main routes through the city centre down High Street.

This first part of the journey is entirely on a reserved formation; however, progress is relatively slow as stops come in quick succession and there are a couple of road crossings to negotiate. Tram drivers must also pay particular attention for pedestrians crossing the tram tracks in this area.

At Castle Square the former "hole in the road" was infilled ahead of the tramway's construction and the area was pedestrianised. Castle Square tram stop stands in the centre of this former Sheffield landmark. A 1985 plan for the light rail system indicates that the "hole" could have been retained and the tram line would have been carried across its north side via a bridge. The nearest stop would have instead been located on High Street near the lower end of Fargate.

Continuing downhill towards Park Square the line crosses Angel Street and Haymarket, then arrives at Fitzalan Square/Ponds Forge. Located in Commercial Street, this is the nearest stop to Sheffield Interchange and is the last before the Halfway and Meadowhall lines diverge. It is often busy with people changing trams, but because of the limited space (the outbound platform is part of the pavement) it lacks real-time information displays.

Commercial Street was a dual carriageway prior to the construction of Supertram, but because of the need for the new tram line to avoid Park Square roundabout, one of the most important road junctions in the city, its eastbound side has been taken over by the tramway. At the bottom of Commercial Street a 70 m bowstring arch bridge carries the line into the centre of Park Square.

Below: Cathedral is one of the busiest stops of the Supertram network, being the city centre terminus of both the Purple Route and, since 2018, tram-train services from Parkgate. On 1 November 2019 399 203 departs from Cathedral with a service for Parkgate, whilst on the left 121 leaves with a Blue Route service to Malin Bridge. **Ian Beardsley**

SOUTH YORKSHIRE SUPERTRAM ROUTES

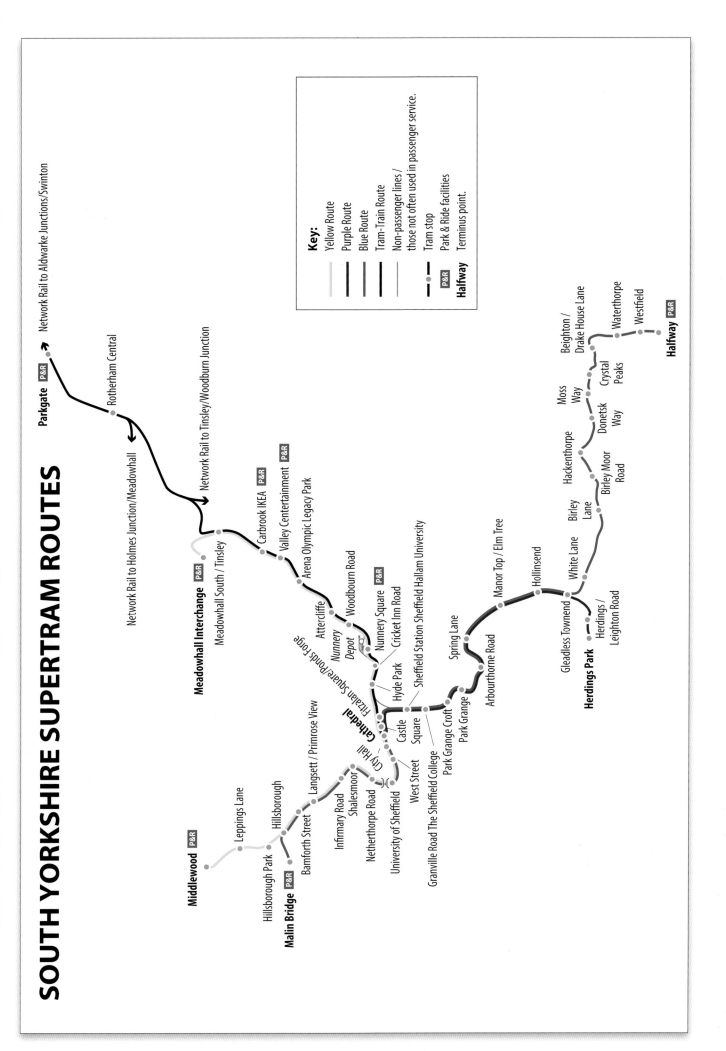

Key:

	Yellow Route
	Purple Route
	Blue Route
	Tram-Train Route
	Non-passenger lines / those not often used in passenger service.
	Tram stop
P&R	Park & Ride facilities
Halfway	Terminus point.

Network Rail to Aldwarke Junctions/Swinton

Parkgate P&R

Rotherham Central

Network Rail to Holmes Junction/Meadowhall

Network Rail to Tinsley/Woodburn Junction

Meadowhall Interchange P&R

Meadowhall South / Tinsley

Carbrook IKEA P&R

Valley Centertainment P&R

Arena Olympic Legacy Park

Attercliffe

Woodbourn Road

Nunnery Depot

Nunnery Square P&R

Cricket Inn Road

Hyde Park

Sheffield Station Sheffield Hallam University

Spring Lane

Manor Top / Elm Tree

Hollinsend

White Lane

Birley Lane

Hackenthorpe

Birley Moor Road

Donetsk Way

Moss Way

Crystal Peaks

Beighton / Drake House Lane

Waterthorpe

Westfield

Halfway P&R

Gleadless Townend

Herdings / Leighton Road

Herdings Park

Arbourthorne Road

Park Grange

Park Grange Croft

Granville Road The Sheffield College

University of Sheffield

West Street

City Hall

Castle Square

Cathedral

Fitzalan Square/Ponds Forge

Netherthorpe Road

Shalesmoor

Infirmary Road

Langsett / Primrose View

Bamforth Street

Hillsborough

Hillsborough Park

Malin Bridge P&R

Leppings Lane

Middlewood P&R

THEN & NOW

From Cathedral Supertram briefly follows one of the original Sheffield Corporation Tramways routes down High Street. Much has changed since the closure of the original system in 1960; however, there are some parts of the street scene that are still recognisable.

Above: On 17 March 1956 Brush/Cravens "Rocker Panel" car 441 approaches the junction of High Street and Market Place with a service bound for Bridge Street. **Howard Turner**

Below: On 1 November 2019 Siemens-Duewag car 119 is pictured at the same location with a Purple Route service for Herdings Park. The former Sheffield Telegraph and Star building, built in 1916 in the Baroque Revival style, still stands on the left. It is now Grade II listed, as is the former bank on the right, which was built around 1900 in the Classic Revival style. It is now a Wetherspoons pub and is appropriately named The Bankers Draft. **Ian Beardsley**

Above: Slightly further down High Street now, in this undated view Brush/Cravens "Rocker Panel" car 487 is seen picking up passengers outside the C&A store. In the background can be seen car 149 built by W. Hill & Co of South Shields and, behind it, the Midland Bank, the corner of which is seen in the previous photograph. **Howard Turner**

Below: Despite the intervening years the scene has changed relatively little. In this 1 November 2019 view Siemens-Duewag car 122 descends High Street with a Halfway-bound Blue Route service. The former C&A, behind the tram, is now an easyHotel. **Ian Beardsley**

Left: 108 comes off the bowstring bridge at Park Square on 2 June 2015. **Paul Jackson**

Right: 113 crosses South Street Viaduct on 23 July 2012 with a service to Cathedral. The Grade II listed Park Hill flats, part of which had then been recently refurbished, dominates the background. The slogan "I love you. Will you marry me?" was inspired by a message graffitied onto a 13th floor footbridge between the flats in 2001. The chimney in the centre of the photo led from the incinerator that used to burn domestic waste from the flats. The heat generated by the incinerator was used to heat water and radiators in the flats complex.
Robert Pritchard

Left: Leaving the city centre trams for Halfway or Herdings Park run alongside Sheffield railway station. On 7 February 2009 tram 108 is seen here heading for Halfway. Class 144 and 150 DMUs are visible in the station.
Robert Pritchard

Above: Car 18 runs along the former Granville Street behind Sheffield station on 29 October 1995 with a Malin Bridge–Herdings Park Orange Route service. Taken from a slightly different viewpoint, the 8 September 1991 view (**below**) shows the area prior to the construction of Supertram. It is highly unusual for a road to be closed with the construction of a tramway; however, as a no through route this served little purpose to road users other than as somewhere to park their cars. **Paul Jackson (2)**

As trams head towards the suburbs on Park Grange Road there are some excellent views over the city. Tram 110 heads towards Halfway on 7 February 2009. Visible behind it is Sheffield United's Bramall Lane football ground, the Royal Hallamshire Hospital and Sheffield University's Arts Tower, then the tallest building in the city. **Robert Pritchard**

Right: 118 descends City Road on 16 September 2014 with a Blue Route service bound for Malin Bridge. Being on the former Intake route, this is one of several parts of the city that were served by the original Sheffield trams; however, under the early plans for the light rail system, Supertram would have instead run through the Manor Estate. **Paul Jackson**

Above: Due to limited space both the inbound and outbound lines run on-street between the stops for Gleadless Townend and Hollinsend. Still wearing its Stagecoach white livery, 117 approaches Hollinsend on 13 July 2007. **Paul Jackson**

Turning right at the delta junction the line crosses a single-span concrete bridge and runs along Granville Street above Sheffield railway station. The platforms for the original tram stop here (closed October 2002) are still extant, but now disused. A newer stop named Sheffield Station Sheffield Hallam University is situated adjacent to the footbridge across from the station. On the hill behind the stop, in South Street Park, is Sheffield Amphitheatre. This was opened in September 2011 as part of a wider regeneration scheme and is used for various outdoor events such as theatrical performances or cinema screenings.

From the station the line continues southwards and crosses Shrewsbury Road, after which is the first short section of on-street running. Granville Road The Sheffield College stop has staggered platforms, the inbound one being passed on the right-hand side before crossing Granville Road; the outbound platform is situated just beyond this steeply graded street, adjacent to Sheffield College's City Campus.

Past Granville Road the line starts to climb and crosses Norfolk Park Road Viaduct, climbing at a gradient of 1 in 20 to come out near Park Grange Road. Without the viaduct the line's ruling 10% gradient would have been exceeded.

Now travelling south-east, the line continues on a reserved formation until just after Park Grange Croft, which opened in 2001 and was named by local residents. The route then follows Park Grange Road, including a short section at 1 in 12, through the Norfolk Park Estate. There are further stops at Park Grange, Arbourthorne Road and Spring Lane. At the time of its planning, it was expected that many Supertram users would come from the Norfolk Park tower blocks; however, these were demolished in the late 1990s/early 2000s and although they have since been replaced by new properties, a greater proportion of the residents are now car owners.

The route briefly levels out around Spring Lane and then turns right to join City Road, running along the former Intake tram route up to Manor Top. From here the line turns right and joins Ridgeway Road, Sheffield's outer ring road. The platforms at Manor Top/Elm Tree are on a short stretch of reserved formation (stopping trams would cause too much disruption to the flow of traffic on this busy road) and from here it was planned that the tram line would continue on a segregated formation along the dual carriageway's central reservation. It was found, however, that there was not sufficient room to do this without uprooting most of the roadside trees. The outbound track thus shares the outer lane of Ridgeway Road, but the inbound track runs on a reserved alignment from Hollinsend. Both this and the Gleadless Townend stops are located on reserved sections in the centre of the dual carriageway.

At Gleadless Townend the Halfway and Herdings lines diverge. To get to Herdings we must therefore alight and await a Purple Route service. Just beyond the tram stop the Halfway line turns left (south-east) onto White Lane, whilst the Herdings line carries straight on onto Norton Avenue. After almost 600 m the Herdings line leaves the road alignment and veers right to run through an open space, the two lines converging just after Herdings/Leighton Road, which roughly marks the highest point of the network – 212.09 m above sea level. From the city centre the line climbs some 143.65 m.

Beyond Herdings/Leighton Road the single track runs west for approximately 460 m to the terminus at Herdings Park. There is no dedicated car parking here, although a nearby bus stop on Raeburn Road offers connections to other areas of the Sheffield suburbs. Like those stops in the Norfolk Park area, it was envisaged that Herdings Park would be popular with residents of the "Three Sisters" tower blocks; however, in October 1996, just 18 months after the line was opened, one of these towers (Raeburn) was demolished after being declared unsafe. The other two blocks, Morland and Leighton – now Queen Anne Court and Queen Elizabeth Court, were subsequently emptied for refurbishment, this coming as a further blow to the line's passenger figures at the time.

Left: Beyond Gleadless Townend the Herdings line runs on-street along Ridgeway Road and Norton Avenue, veering off onto a short section of segregated formation from Herdings/Leighton Road to the terminus at Herdings Park. On 18 September 2019 115 is seen on the approach to Herdings/Leighton Road on Norton Avenue. **Ian Beardsley**

Above: The short single track section on the Herdings Park line makes for a very rural scene as 110 approaches Herdings/Leighton Road heading for Meadowhall, via Cathedral, on 29 March 2013. **Paul Jackson**

Left: 117 stands at Herdings Park terminus on the evening of 18 September 2019 prior to working the 18.17 service to Cathedral. Situated in a relatively remote location, this stop has been the scene of a number of crimes in the past and it also suffers from vandalism, with Supertram services sometimes being disrupted as a result. **Ian Beardsley**

Having returned to Gleadless Townend we cross platforms and await a Blue Route service to Halfway. These are timetabled to run every 12 minutes during off-peak hours.

Leaving Gleadless Townend the tram takes a left and follows White Lane, running on-street as far as what was formerly The Old Harrow public house, now an Indian Restaurant. Just beyond here is the county boundary. On entering Derbyshire trams run approximately 900 m through farmland on ballasted track, eventually coming back into Sheffield on Birley Lane. A tram stop here serves the neighbouring residential area and also Birley Academy.

On-street running resumes just below Birley Lane tram stop, near the Fairway public house and the entrance to Birley Wood Golf Club (on the right). It is not unusual, particularly in foggy conditions, to see road vehicles travelling in the opposite direction which have overshot here and ended up stuck on the ballast! But for reserved sections at Birley Moor Road and Hackenthorpe tram stops, the outbound track runs on-street as far as Donetsk Way; the inbound line has an additional section of segregated track alongside Birley Lane. From Donetsk Way to Halfway the alignment is entirely on a reserved formation, either running alongside roads or across fields. There are, however, multiple road crossings, which can slow the progress of trams.

Beyond Birley the route descends into an area that was developed in the late 1980s/early 1990s as a satellite township of Sheffield, known collectively as Mosborough. Tram stops at Donetsk Way and Moss Way serve the nearby residential areas, whilst Crystal Peaks tram stop serves the shopping centre of the same name. Located on the edge of the retail development, this also serves the area of Waterthorpe, and people living further afield can change for local bus services from Crystal Peaks bus station.

After curving around the edge of the shopping centre trams come to Beighton/Drake House Lane, which is the nearest stop to the village of Beighton. People may also alight here to access the opposite end of Crystal Peaks. Leaving the stop the line turns almost 90° to head south alongside Eckington Way, which it parallels as far as Halfway terminus, the site of a 190-space Park & Ride car park and also the terminus of several bus routes. Local residents, students of Westfield School and workers in the nearby industrial estate benefit from intermediate stops at Waterthorpe and Westfield.

Above: 120 is seen heading into Sheffield at Gleadless Townend on 12 February 2011. Here the two tracks of the Halfway route are briefly separated by a group of buildings, the inbound line bearing left to meet the line from Herdings whilst the outbound line, which takes a sharp left immediately after Gleadless Townend tram stop, comes in from the right. **Paul Jackson**

Above: 107 is pictured on the approach to Hackenthorpe on 16 February 2011. **Paul Jackson**

Left: A short section of the Halfway route between White Lane and Birley Lane runs through north-east Derbyshire. Tram 105 is seen on this section of line on a snowy 7 February 2009. **Robert Pritchard**

Stadler tram-train 207 pauses at the Birley Moor Road stop with a Blue Route service to Malin Bridge on 3 August 2019. **Alan Yearsley**

Left: With part of the shopping centre in the background, 114 arrives at Crystal Peaks with a Blue Route service to Malin Bridge on 14 September 2019. **Alan Yearsley**

Above: 117 passes Crystal Peaks shopping centre on 21 March 2014. **Paul Jackson**

Left: 123 negotiates the 90° curve and the gradient into the Beighton/Drake House Lane stop on 14 September 2019. **Alan Yearsley**

39

THE MIDDLEWOOD/MALIN BRIDGE LINE

Having returned into the city centre from Halfway we can continue on a Blue Route service through to the terminus at Malin Bridge. Again sitting in the direction of travel, the cathedral is now on the right, whilst on the left is the Grade II listed Cutlers' Hall. Dating from 1832 and now the third such building to occupy the site, the Cutlers' Hall is described as one of the finest livery halls in the North of England. Nowadays it is used for a variety of public and private events including concerts, dances, lectures and weddings.

Departing from the Cathedral stop trams join Church Street and follow the road, and indeed the former tram route to Crookes and

Walkley, up West Street and Glossop Road. The desire for Supertram to serve the University of Sheffield has meant that the route is far from direct. Sheffield Corporation Tramways services to Middlewood and Malin Bridge turned off at what is now Castle Square and ran down Angel Street, reaching Shalesmoor via Snig Hill, West Bar and Gibraltar Street.

At the junction with Upper Hanover Street, part of Sheffield's inner ring road, trams leave the former Crookes route and turn sharp right to reach the University of Sheffield stop. This is located on a reserved formation in the centre of the dual carriageway, nearby the university's Jessop West campus and its main library, the Information Commons.

121 descends Church Street as it approaches the Cathedral stop with a service for Meadowhall on 16 July 2007. **Paul Jackson**

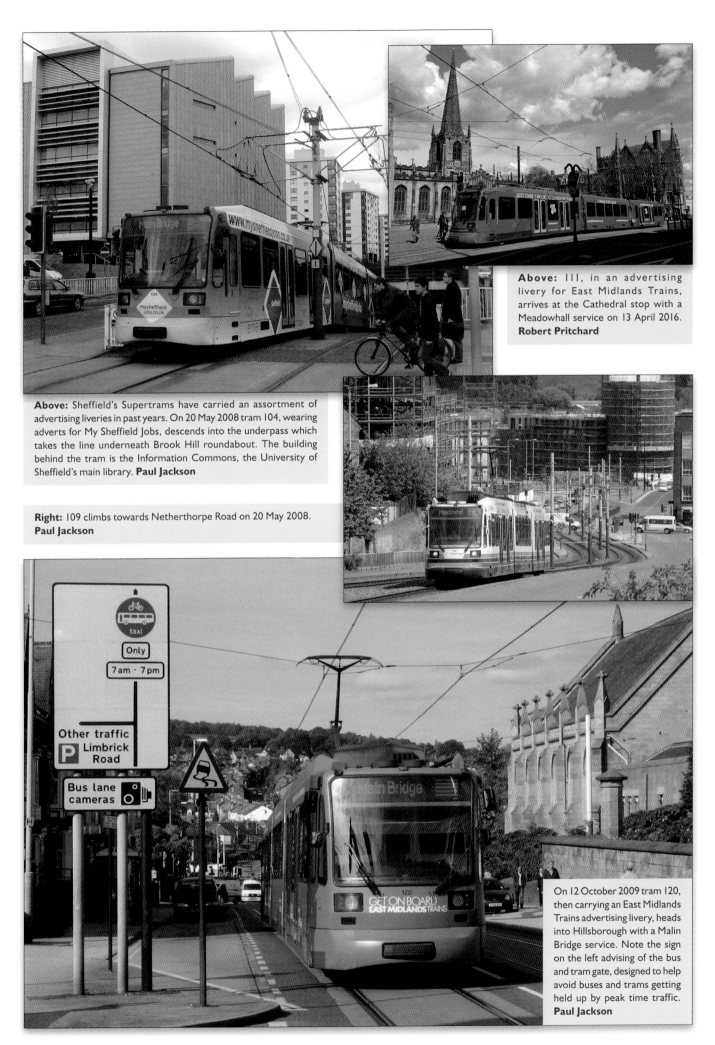

Above: 111, in an advertising livery for East Midlands Trains, arrives at the Cathedral stop with a Meadowhall service on 13 April 2016. **Robert Pritchard**

Above: Sheffield's Supertrams have carried an assortment of advertising liveries in past years. On 20 May 2008 tram 104, wearing adverts for My Sheffield Jobs, descends into the underpass which takes the line underneath Brook Hill roundabout. The building behind the tram is the Information Commons, the University of Sheffield's main library. **Paul Jackson**

Right: 109 climbs towards Netherthorpe Road on 20 May 2008. **Paul Jackson**

On 12 October 2009 tram 120, then carrying an East Midlands Trains advertising livery, heads into Hillsborough with a Malin Bridge service. Note the sign on the left advising of the bus and tram gate, designed to help avoid buses and trams getting held up by peak time traffic. **Paul Jackson**

A short walk is required to access most other parts of the university such as its Students' Union on Brook Hill, just below Sheffield Children's Hospital.

Immediately north of the University of Sheffield stop is Brook Hill roundabout. To avoid disrupting traffic, trams pass beneath this in an underpass. As we leave the stop and descend into the underpass note the former Henderson's Relish factory (now owned by the university and planned to be converted into a public house) on the right-hand side on Leavygreave Road.

Trams emerge from the Brook Hill underpass in the central reservation of Netherthorpe Road, the continuation of the inner ring road. Because of the limited space in the centre of the dual carriageway an island platform is provided at Netherthorpe Road. This is accessed via a subway at the south-western end of the stop. Heading towards the city's northern suburbs the line continues onto Hoyle Street and curves left to regain the original tram route towards Middlewood and Malin Bridge, following this on-street north-west along Infirmary Road and Langsett Road. There are further stops at Shalesmoor, Infirmary Road, Langsett/Primrose View, Bamforth Street and Hillsborough.

As per the recommendations of the S/RLUTS, Penistone Road was converted to a dual carriageway in the late 1980s/early 1990s with the intention that the parallel Supertram route could be for the sole use of public transport or providing access. Bus/tram gates were subsequently introduced near the centre of Hillsborough; however, many road users complained that the signs were unclear and the City Council had to remove the restrictions and issue refunds to thousands of drivers who had been fined. The signage has since been amended and the restrictions reintroduced.

At Hillsborough Corner the short Malin Bridge branch turns left (south-east) onto Holme Lane, whilst the Middlewood line continues north-west on Middlewood Road. The branch runs entirely on-street and terminates before Malin Bridge itself in the centre of a residential area. A small Park & Ride car park (with 104 spaces) is provided opposite the tram stop, and there are nearby bus stops with connections to Stannington and Low Bradfield.

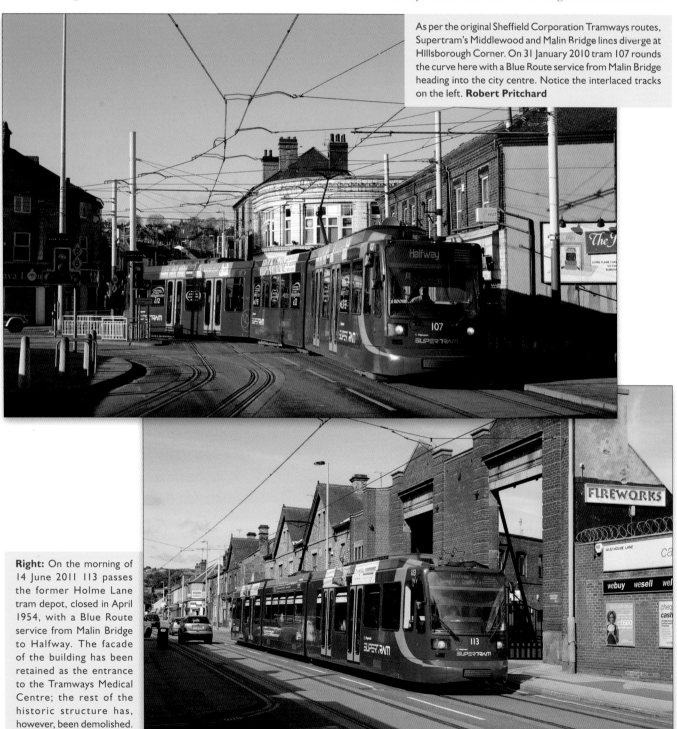

As per the original Sheffield Corporation Tramways routes, Supertram's Middlewood and Malin Bridge lines diverge at Hillsborough Corner. On 31 January 2010 tram 107 rounds the curve here with a Blue Route service from Malin Bridge heading into the city centre. Notice the interlaced tracks on the left. **Robert Pritchard**

Right: On the morning of 14 June 2011 113 passes the former Holme Lane tram depot, closed in April 1954, with a Blue Route service from Malin Bridge to Halfway. The facade of the building has been retained as the entrance to the Tramways Medical Centre; the rest of the historic structure has, however, been demolished. **Robert Pritchard**

Sheffield Corporation-liveried 120 arrives at the Malin Bridge terminus on 14 June 2011. As it was originally planned the line to Stannington would have continued along Holme Lane on the left and then up Stannington Road. Inbound trams would have returned towards the city via Loxley Road and then turned right into Loxley New Road, where Malin Bridge terminus is located. A triangle at the junction of Holme Lane, Stannington Road and Loxley Road would have allowed short workings to return to the city without having to reverse. **Robert Pritchard**

Right: 114 departs Middlewood on 14 June 2011. Just beyond the rear of the tram the outbound line takes a sharp right and crosses the carriageway to run on a short stretch of reserved formation into the terminus. A minor incident occurred here on 19 July 2018 when the driver of tram 117 "lost awareness" and failed to reduce the speed of the tram in advance of the 10 mph speed restriction on the curve. As a result passengers were subject to "excessive lateral accelerations" and one suffered serious injuries when she was flung against a set of the exterior doors, causing one of them to come open. A series of safety measures have since been put in place to avoid a repeat. **Robert Pritchard**

A notable feature on this part of the route is the former Holme Lane tram depot, now the Tramways Medical Centre, located approximately half way between Hillsborough and Malin Bridge on the right.

We return to Hillsborough and cross the road to await a Yellow Route service to Middlewood. Like the Malin Bridge branch, beyond Hillsborough Corner the Middlewood line runs on-street throughout, passing Hillsborough Park, which since 2018 has been the venue of Tramlines music festival, on the right. Festivalgoers are advised to use the Hillsborough Corner tram stop, which is an approximately two-minute walk from the venue. There is, however, another tram stop at the north-west corner of the park, Leppings Lane, the staggered platforms of which are regularly used by Sheffield Wednesday supporters attending home games at Hillsborough. After passing the stadium on the right the tram line continues a short distance along Middlewood Road and prior to reaching the terminus the outbound line crosses the road to run on a short stretch of reserved formation, thus preventing the road from being blocked by trams queuing to access the single platform terminus. A 343-space Park & Ride car park is provided at Middlewood and at the time of writing Stagecoach operates two Supertram Link bus services (SL1 and SL1A) to provide fast and frequent connections to Oughtibridge, Deepcar and Stocksbridge.

We return into the city centre and now take the Meadowhall line through the Don Valley.

THE MEADOWHALL LINE

The route to Meadowhall diverges from the Halfway line at a triangular junction at Park Square, just outside the city centre. It bears left and runs along the south side of the Sheffield Parkway on a six-span post-tensioned reinforced concrete segmental viaduct. At 350 m-long this is one of the most impressive structures on the system. A girder bridge carries the tram route over the former Midland Railway line towards Meadowhall, and it then comes to the first of seven road crossings, Bernard Road, immediately after which is Hyde Park tram stop. This serves a number of nearby blocks of flats, which, along with those at Park Hill overlooking the station, were inspired by the "brutalist" style of French architect Le Corbusier and at the time of their construction were considered revolutionary. By the mid 1980s, however, Sheffield City Council considered the Hyde Park flats as a failed experiment in social housing, and two blocks, Hyde Park South and the smaller Hyde Park West, were demolished in the 1990s. The other blocks were refurbished ahead of the World Student Games in 1991 and were temporarily used to house competitors, but later reverted to being social housing.

Beyond Hyde Park the line follows the alignment of the former Aston Street, running alongside, but at a lower level to Cricket Inn Road, which gives its name to the next tram stop. This was once the site of a Park & Ride facility, but the modest car park here was replaced by the much larger one (377 spaces) at nearby Nunnery Square, on the opposite side of the Sheffield Parkway. Leaving Cricket Inn Road the line turns north to cross the Parkway, and then east to run alongside Supertram's Nunnery depot, which was built partly on the site of the London & North Western Railway's engine shed (closed 1928) and

Left: Under a threatening sky on the morning of 20 September 2012 tram 107 heads out of the city centre at Park Square with a Yellow Route service to Meadowhall. **Robert Pritchard**

123 is pictured at the delta junction at Park Square on 10 June 2015, travelling out of service towards the city centre. **Robert Pritchard**

112 crosses Parkway Viaduct on 17 November 2006 with a Yellow Route service towards Meadowhall. In the foreground is Victoria Quays, the terminus of the Sheffield & Tinsley Canal, whilst in the background is the remaining part of Hyde Park West. **Paul Jackson**

Right: Over Easter 2011 rail replacement work took place at the delta junction at Park Square, which gave rise to various unusual tram workings. On Good Friday 22 April that year 108 is pictured coming off the main line and running into Nunnery depot using the eastern access line. It would then proceed along road 7, through the wash, and then along the outbound line to Cricket Inn Road where passengers would alight for rail replacement buses into the city centre. The parapet in the bottom right is that of the bridge that used to carry Woodbourn Road over the London North Western Railway between Woodburn Junction and its City Goods depot at Bernard Road. **Ian Beardsley**

the exchange sidings for Nunnery Colliery. The depot is connected to the main running line via spurs at either end of the site. The former staff halt, just to the south-west of the depot building, now forms the stop for Nunnery Square Park & Ride.

Turning north again, the line crosses the depot access road and then goes over the former Manchester, Sheffield & Lincolnshire Railway (MS&LR – later absorbed into the Great Central Railway and now part of the national rail network) to parallel Woodbourn Road on a reserved formation, crossing it at the junction of Worthing Road and Jessel Street to reach Woodbourn Road tram stop, which serves this largely industrial part of the city. The tram tracks continue to follow Woodbourn Road, but now on its right-hand side, as far as its junction with Staniforth Road. The crossing here has been the site of a number of accidents, the most severe of which was on 25 October 2018 when tram-train 399 204 was derailed in a collision with a flatbed lorry.

Just beyond Staniforth Road the tram line crosses the Sheffield & Tinsley Canal and then curves to the right to reach Attercliffe tram stop, built to serve the neighbouring technology park. Leaving Attercliffe the line crosses Shirland Lane and runs along an embankment next to the canal to join the formation of the MS&LR's Sheffield–Rotherham Central–Doncaster route near to the site of the former Attercliffe station (closed 1927).

Left: 122 approaches Woodbourn Road tram stop on 25 March 2016. Behind the tram can be seen the decorative retaining wall of what is now Sheffield Hallam University's City Athletics Stadium. Previously known as Woodburn Stadium, this closed in 2011, but later reopened following a £325 000 refurbishment as a replacement for the nearby Don Valley Stadium, which was controversially closed in September 2013 and subsequently demolished as Sheffield City Council sought to slash its annual budget by almost £50 million. The unusual waved pattern on the wall was financed through Government money made available to the City Council for environmental enhancements associated with the Supertram project. **Paul Jackson**

Right: 05 crosses the bridge over the Sheffield & Tinsley Canal on 7 May 1994. The bridge was inspired by that which is found at Ironbridge Gorge, the world's first iron bridge. On the Meadowhall side of the structure is a footbridge that was also built as part of the Supertram scheme. **Paul Jackson**

Below: An unidentified tram passes the Sheffield & Tinsley Canal at Attercliffe on 6 October 2008. The canal opened in 1819 and it was in daily use up until the late 1960s, but nowadays this peaceful stretch of inland waterway is solely used by pleasure craft. The former winding hole here was remodelled as part of the construction of the Supertram system to provide a new leisure facility for canal users, with a small landing stage being constructed at the base of the large retaining wall on the left. This has, however, since fallen into a state of disrepair. **Paul Jackson**

At one time this route was exceptionally busy with freight traffic moving to and from Tinsley Marshalling Yard; however, much of this dwindled with the run down of rail freight in Britain in the 1980s and with the construction of Supertram the line was singled. At the time of writing there are only a handful of workings booked to use the route each day, most of which are freight trains, but a couple of passenger services also run this way in order for drivers to retain route knowledge. Services to and from the North are occasionally diverted via this route in the event of any engineering works or disruption on the main line through Meadowhall.

After crossing Worksop Road (note the railway bridge and canal aqueduct to the right) the tram line runs alongside the Olympic Legacy Park, a combination of world class sporting, educational and research facilities that partly occupy the site of Don Valley Stadium. This is also home to the Sheffield Eagles rugby club. Tram users can access the facilities, and also the English Institute of Sport, Don Valley Bowl and Sheffield Arena, by taking a short walk from the Arena Olympic Legacy Park tram stop (known as Arena/Don Valley until late 2017).

Passing the 13 600 capacity arena on the left, home to the Sheffield Steelers ice hockey club, trams bound for Meadowhall continue under Broughton Lane and then come to Valley Centertainment, a leisure and entertainment complex. Opened on 5 November 1998, the site boasts a number of restaurants, a bowling alley, adventure golf and laser quest; however, the major attraction here is the Cineworld cinema, one of the busiest in the country with over 20 screens. A new tram

stop and 200 space car park were provided with the opening of the complex to form a new Park & Ride. Behind the inbound platform is Broughton Lane Junction where one of the lines into Tinsley Yard branches off from the Woodburn Junction–Rotherham Central route.

The next stop, less than 400 m away, is Carbrook IKEA. Originally titled Carbrook, this was built to serve Meadowhall Retail Park, but in 2017 it was renamed in connection with the opening of the adjacent Swedish furniture store. Like at Centertainment, 167 Park & Ride spaces were provided in connection with this development. At both locations staff monitor Park & Ride users to ensure that they park in the allocated spaces. Supertram was keen to encourage use of the tram to get to IKEA, but in its publicity at the time cautioned people that there were restrictions on just how much could be taken on board!

At the far end of the IKEA car park the tram route passes underneath the route of the former Sheffield District Railway, which linked the Midland Railway's Sheffield–Rotherham line to the Chesterfield–Rotherham "Old Road" via junctions at Brightside and Treeton, giving the Lancashire, Derbyshire & East Coast Railway (LD&ECR) access into Sheffield Midland. Through running powers it also enabled the Great Eastern Railway to access the Sheffield freight facilities. Passenger services over the route (to Mansfield via the LD&ECR's Beighton branch, and Chesterfield via the "Old Road") ceased in September 1939. The latter service was briefly revived from October 1946 to March 1947, however. Freight services lasted much longer, but the line between Tinsley Yard and Treeton was closed in

Left: Much of the Meadowhall route is on former heavy rail alignments. On 5th February tram 104 is seen having just left Arena/Don Valley whilst working a Yellow Route service towards Middlewood. Alongside, on the former MS&LR route between Sheffield and Rotherham, Cross Country Voyagers 221 136 and 220 015 head in the opposite direction with the diverted 09.25 Plymouth–Dundee service. **Ian Beardsley**

Right: Don Valley Stadium and Sheffield Arena were two major projects undertaken in connection with the 1991 World Student Games (Universiade). A tram stop was constructed near Coleridge Road to jointly serve the two facilities, but its opening was delayed as the requirements for handling large crowds at sports grounds set out in the Lord Justice Taylor's report into the Hillsborough Disaster had not been met by the time the Meadowhall line opened. On 4 September 1994 spectators return home after an athletics event at Don Valley Stadium. **Paul Jackson**

THEN & NOW

Left: Seen here on 16 April 1997, with tram 21 in the foreground crossing the River Don bridge, the cooling towers of the former Blackburn Meadows Power Station were for many years a notable feature on the Sheffield skyline and often appear in the background of photographs of trams in the Meadowhall area; however, they were controversially demolished in the early hours of 24 August 2008, 27 years after the power station closed. **Paul Jackson**

Right: 22 years on the scene has changed somewhat. Tram-train 399 206 approaches Meadowhall South on 24 March 2019. Behind it is the bridge over the River Don and just after that the tram-train route takes a sharp right to head towards Rotherham. The Meadowhall line bears slightly left and runs alongside the viaduct, which carries the M1 motorway. **Robert Pritchard**

Left: As trams approach Meadowhall South they diverge from the former MS&LR route towards Rotherham and take the formation of the SYR Barnsley branch to run over the River Don and then alongside the Tinsley Viaduct. On 10 October 2008 car 102, which is bound for Middlewood, is seen having just passed the site of the former Tinsley South Junction. **Paul Jackson**

Right: As it once was: Tinsley South Junction on 3 October 1984. Like at other locations, much has changed in the intervening years, but the location is still recognisable from the M1 viaduct in the background and the industrial unit on the left. **Paul Jackson**

Left: Another photographic location which has been lost to vegetation growth: On 6 December 2008 tram 105, with a Purple Route service to Herdings Park, drops down onto the former alignment of the South Yorkshire Railway's Barnsley branch near Meadowhall. In the background is the M1 Tinsley Viaduct. Built from steel box girders, it was the first such structure of its kind in the UK. At the time of its construction in the mid to late 1960s most other long span bridges were built to a post-tensioned concrete deck design; this, however, was expected to be much cheaper, the build costing a mere £6 million! Three serious disasters with similar structures in the early 1970s prompted several programmes of strengthening works, the most recent of which cost £82 million – almost 14 times the original budget!
Robert Pritchard

Right: The terminus of the Meadowhall line is alongside the bus and railway stations here, allowing tram users to easily access other parts of the area and even further afield. 1002 is pictured at Meadowhall Interchange on 17 September 1993. On the left an unidentified High Speed Train heads towards Sheffield.
Paul Jackson

1993; that between Brightside and Shepcote Lane Junction was taken out of use in 1992.

The 1090 m from Carbrook to Meadowhall South/Tinsley is the longest section on the Supertram network between stops and, not having any road crossings or sharp curves to restrict their speed, is also usually the only section where trams can reach their maximum speed of 50 mph. Just before reaching Meadowhall South the tram line leaves the Network Rail route towards Rotherham Central (near Tinsley South Junction) and takes the alignment of the former South Yorkshire Railway's (SYR) Barnsley branch (closed under British Rail ownership in 1988) to run alongside the M1 Tinsley Viaduct. Meadowhall South/Tinsley is conveniently located for the House of Fraser and Debenhams department stores in the nearby shopping centre, but passengers for Meadowhall often choose to travel through to the terminus as there is an undercover walking route leading directly from the interchange into the shopping complex. The residential area of Tinsley is a short walk away and can be accessed via the canal towpath.

Immediately after crossing the River Don the tram-train route veers off to the right to rejoin the Network Rail line at Tinsley North Junction. The tram line continues parallel to the M1. Prior to crossing Alsing Road, at the site of Tinsley West Junction the two tracks merge. The single track then climbs and turns sharply left to run south-west alongside Network Rail's Sheffield–Rotherham main line, terminating at Meadowhall Interchange to offer connections with national rail and local bus services. The 16-stand bus station is also served by long-distance coach operators, and the station features a 328-space Park & Ride car park; its proximity to the M1 means that it is easily accessed via the road network.

Largely using former heavy rail routes, there are few severe gradients on the Meadowhall line. Between Park Square and Nunnery there are some stretches of 1 in 20, and after crossing the railway it falls at 1 in 12.5 to meet Woodbourn Road. But for another brief stretch of 1 in 20 where the tramway climbs from the alignment of the former SYR to run alongside the Sheffield–Rotherham line, from Attercliffe to the terminus at Meadowhall the maximum gradient is 1 in 62 – almost level by light rail standards!

INFRASTRUCTURE

Work across the network included the construction of two large viaducts, nine bridges, an underpass and around 50 other structures, most of which were retaining walls. An estimated 1750 tonnes of structural steelwork, 4000 tonnes of reinforcement steelwork and 23 000 cubic metres of concrete were used in the project, along with 120 km of rail.

TRACKWORK

The Supertram system features two types of track – tramway track, which is shared with road vehicles and pedestrians, and ballasted track, where there is no such requirement.

Tramway track

Tramway track consists of a grooved tramway rail set into a 2.2 m-wide concrete base with two approximately 192 mm-wide and 165 mm-deep channels into which the rails are laid. In order to construct the on-street sections in the shortest possible time and thus minimise disruption, Balfour Beatty opted to use a slip-form paver to produce this concrete base. Although widely used in the production of roads, kerbs and airport runways, this method had never before been used in tramway construction.

The process entails ready-mixed concrete, mixed to a specified tolerance, being poured from a lorry onto a conveyor feeding into a screw. The screw then forces the concrete, via a series of vibrating pokers, under the body of the machine to the steel formwork which produces grooved concrete. This is then hand floated and brushed to provide an anti-skid surface, after which it is sprayed with an aluminium-resin curing agent. When paving is interrupted and the concrete is allowed to dry, the former will no longer fit into the channels and a small gap therefore has to be left to be filled in later.

In a typical eight-hour day up to 250 m of concrete trackbed could be produced using the slip-form paver, with a lorry load of six cubic metres of ready-mixed concrete being required every six metres. By comparison, only 50–100 m of concrete trackbed can be produced per day using the traditional formwork shuttering method.

The tramway rail can be laid into the grooves after four or five days. Rails are first laid on top of the concrete bed and to prevent rail web oscillation and hence provide a quiet ride, they are made into a solid mass by attaching 400 mm-long pre-formed concrete blocks into the web. These are then fixed using an adhesive. The rails are welded together using the Thermit process, and are cross-bonded for electrical purposes. Pipes are laid during the production of the concrete slab to accommodate these bonding wires, which are welded to the rail webs before they are lowered into the channels. Finally the bottom and sides of the grooves are packed every metre to ensure that the rails will be correctly aligned, the rails are inserted into the channels, and set into an adhesive compound.

Edilon Corkelast VO, a solvent-free polyurethane adhesive incorporating cork, was originally used, with a neat solution being poured to just above the foot of the rail and dilute being used from

Left: A slip-former in use on City Road producing the concrete base into which the grooved tramway rails are laid. The operative is trowelling the surface as the machine progresses along the road. **Peter Fox**

Right: A concrete former on Park Grange Road as produced by the slip-former. The steel reinforcement can be seen in the foreground. **Peter Fox**

Left: The first tramway rails to be installed in the city since the closure of the original tram network await installation at the Woodbourn Road crossing. Prior to being laid into the concrete troughing, concrete blocks would be affixed to the rail webs to reduce the amount of polymer required to set them in place. **Peter Fox**

Right: Concrete blocks are strapped to the grooved tramway rails ahead of their installation at Woodbourn Road crossing. **Paul Jackson**

Below: Ballasted railway track at Halfway. The rails are fixed to the sleepers, most of which are concrete blocks with steel ties, by means of Pandrol clips. In the foreground there are a few wooden sleepers, onto which the Vehicle Identification System (VIS) loop is mounted. **Ian Beardsley**

there to the surface. It was later found that the compound was prone to debonding and also of low skid resistance, thus posing a risk to motor vehicles. The top 25 mm was subsequently replaced with aluminium hydride compound mixed with bauxite chippings, and this has since been used for full depth embedment during the various rail replacement projects. Astorstag compound has also been used.

SEI 35G grooved rail, manufactured by British Steel and SOGA, France, was used during the construction of the system. It has since been replaced by rail with the similar profile SEI 35GP, whilst more recent rail replacement work has seen 55G2 grooved rails with the SEI 41GP profile installed. These latter rails have a wider and deeper groove, allowing the Stadler Citylink tram-trains used on Cathedral–Parkgate services to be operated over other parts of the Supertram network. Produced from premium grade steels, they have also been metallurgically designed to give a longer life than the rails that were used previously.

Rail grooves are drained using standard Balfour Beatty drain boxes, which are connected to the street drainage system. Rodding boxes are incorporated into the system to assist with cleaning.

The grooved rail sections have no fixed lubrication system.

Ballasted track

Where trams run on a segregated alignment, for example on the Meadowhall line, ballasted track is usually used on a prepared formation. Upon construction this consisted of BS11-80A flat bottom rail, sourced from British Steel Track Products of Workington, mounted on twin block sleepers with steel ties, and held in place with pandrol clips. Wooden sleepers are found where there are any expansion joints. Rail joints are connected using fishplates.

Street crossings in areas of ballasted track can use either railway rail, with a steel section alongside to provide an edge for the concrete, or grooved tramway rails.

Fixed "plunger" type lubrication units are installed on the single track curve at Meadowhall, both tracks on the curve at Broughton Lane and on the inbound line near the Parkway bridge. Partec canisters are also used to provide lubrication in other areas, generally on sharp curves where there are check rails fitted.

POINTWORK

Turnouts, most of which are 25 m radius, are similarly constructed with the type of rail varying according to their location. For heavy duty crossings specially cast manganese steel is employed for durability; for the remainder 39E1 flat-bottom rail is used. The method of trackbed construction and rail fixing is largely the same as with plain track; however, the concrete bed had to be hand-cast for those points with grooved rails.

Above: To help improve ride quality and extend the life of the infrastructure, rail grinders are used to smooth and remove defective metals from the railhead. SPENO rail grinder HRR 12-M1 is seen on Glossop Road looking towards the University of Sheffield tram stop on 27 May 1997. This ran wrong line from Glossop Road to Commercial Street. On the right is a Metro Cammell Weymann Metrobus on route 60. **Paul Jackson**

The system uses a combination of spring return, motor operated and unpowered turnouts. All grooved track turnouts are equipped with Hanning & Kahl type HWE 60 electro-hydraulic point setting mechanisms. Ballasted track turnouts on the main line use Hanning & Kahl type HWE 150 electro-hydraulic units. Unpowered turnouts in the depot use Balfour Beatty point machines.

ELECTRIFICATION

Overhead line equipment is used to supply trams with a nominal 750 V DC supply from 12 electricity substations around the network. Located at Blackburn Meadows, Carbrook, Nunnery, Middlewood, Langsett Road, University, Park Square, Arbourthorne, Gleadless, Birley, Crystal Peaks and Halfway, these convert the 11 kV AC supply and feed the DC output into the system's almost 120 km of contact wire. Consisting of twin 107 mm cadmium copper wires, made necessary because of the high installed power rating of the Siemens trams, the contact wire

Above: Tram 113 departs Waterthorpe on 15 May 2010 with a Blue Route service bound for Malin Bridge. In places such as this where the tram tracks are situated close together masts are usually placed between the two tracks and spans either side hold the contact wire roughly above the centre of each line. To even out pantograph head wear the contact wire is positioned slightly differently at each span, this effectively creating a zigzag pattern when viewed from above or below. **Robert Pritchard**

DIAGRAM OF POWER SUPPLY SYSTEM

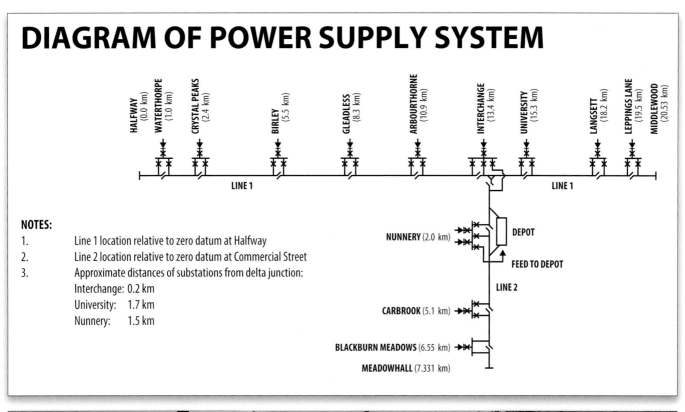

NOTES:

1. Line 1 location relative to zero datum at Halfway
2. Line 2 location relative to zero datum at Commercial Street
3. Approximate distances of substations from delta junction:
   Interchange: 0.2 km
   University: 1.7 km
   Nunnery: 1.5 km

Where possible, in the city centre building fixings are used to support the overhead wires. In this busy scene at High Street on 12 August 2018, we see support masts on the left, with lightweight nylon ropes connecting to the buildings on the right. **Ian Beardsley**

is held approximately five to six metres above the railhead, its height varying depending upon location. There are some 2300 supports, poles or building fixtures across the system. Where the two tracks are close together, as on the Meadowhall line, usually a central pole is used with arms either side, whilst on sections of on-street running there are masts on either side of the carriageway with lightweight nylon span ropes between them. For maximum environmental and aesthetic benefit building fixtures are used wherever possible,

particularly in the city centre. OLE structures in the vicinity of tram stops bear the appropriate three letter code (e.g. SHQ for Cathedral) and numbers. Pole 0000 is situated in the centre of the delta junction at Park Square.

The network's power supply is controlled from the Nunnery depot using the computer-based Supervisory Control and Data Acquisition (SCADA) system, which was supplied by Transmitton Ltd, a division of Balfour Beatty.

SIGNALLING

Movements over most of the Supertram system are performed using "line of sight" driving. This requires tram drivers to maintain a speed such that they can stop short of any obstructions using only the normal service brakes. Track brakes are also fitted for use in the event of an emergency. Some signalling is, however, required on the various single line sections, at road crossings, and in areas of on-street running in order to prevent a collision. Thought was given to also installing block signalling, like that used on the railways, on the segregated section of line between Attercliffe and Meadowall, but this was found to be unnecessary.

In many places trams have priority over normal road traffic and they therefore use a separate system to the conventional red/amber/green traffic lights to avoid confusion. The tram signals consists of five white lights arranged either vertically, allowing the tram to proceed, or horizontally, indicating that the tram should stop. Diagonal lights indicate that a tram may proceed if it is turning left or right. A cross is the equivalent of a normal amber road signal.

Point indicators are used on the approach to junctions to inform drivers of which way points are set. The route that a tram is to take is computer-controlled and can be set using the on-board Vehicle Identification System (VIS) prior to the commencement of each journey. On the approach to junctions a signal is sent via a transponder on the tram to a VIS loop buried beneath the track. The points should automatically then be set for the correct direction. Removable point levers may be used in the event of a system failure. This same system is also used on the approach to road junctions to interface with the computers controlling the traffic light phasing so that trams are given priority over other road users.

In addition to signals, lineside signs are used to give warnings or instructions to tram drivers. Speed restrictions, as agreed with the railway inspectorate, are the most common example. In some cases, for example where there is a sharp curve on the approach to Middlewood, trams will have to adhere to a lower speed than normal road traffic. To avoid causing confusion to other road users tramway signs are diamond shaped.

A warning sign for pedestrians crossing the tram tracks on the former Granville Street. **Ian Beardsley**

Below: 125 pauses at Leppings Lane on 14 June 2011 whilst on a service to Middlewood. Note the tram signal mounted on top of the left-hand traffic light. **Robert Pritchard**

SUPERTRAM SIGNALS & INDICATORS

FIXED SIGNALS

Signals normally display five white lights which are distinctive from those of the standard road traffic lights or railway lineside signals and have the meanings indicated:

STOP

STRAIGHT
THROUGH
TRAM OR TRAIN
MAY PROCEED

LEFT
TURNING TRAM
OR TRAIN MAY
PROCEED

RIGHT
TURNING TRAM
OR TRAIN MAY
PROCEED

THIS IS
EQUIVALENT TO
AN AMBER
ROAD TRAFFIC
LIGHT SIGNAL

POINTS INDICATORS

Points indicators are provided at junctions to indicate the route that is set through points. At junctions where the tram and train movements can conflict with road traffic, fixed signals are provided in addition to points indicators. The aspects displayed by the points indicators are:

STOP
(POINTS MISALIGNED/NOT DETECTED)

POINTS SET FOR LEFT
TURNING TRACK

POINTS SET FOR RIGHT
TURNING TRACK

A points indicator may be passed only if it displays the correct route indication for the tram or train concerned and, where fixed signals are provided, if both points indicators and fixed signals are set for the correct route.

SUPERTRAM SIGNS

STOP AND
PROCEED
WHEN SAFE
TO DO SO

GIVE WAY TO
ANOTHER TRAM,
TRAIN OR
ROAD VEHICLE

MAXIMUM
PERMITTED SPEED
IN MILES
PER HOUR

SOUND
AUDIBLE
WARNING

TEMPORARY SPEED
RESTRICTION

TERMINATION OF
TEMPORARY SPEED
RESTRICTION

INSTRUCTION SIGN
OBSERVE SPECIFIC
INSTRUCTION ON
PLATE BELOW

EXAMPLES OF SPECIFIC INSTRUCTIONS

| S | PREPARE TO STOP AT COMMENCEMENT POINT OF INTERLOCKING AREA |

| SS | INTERLOCKING AREA COMMENCES ("SAFETY SIGNALLING") |

| SS | TERMINATION OF INTERLOCKING AREA |

| I | SECTION GAP |

| LOS | LIMIT OF SHUNT |

NUNNERY DEPOT

The Supertram depot is located on a 2.6 acre site at Nunnery, just outside the city centre, on former railway land adjacent to the Sheffield–Lincoln line. Designed and built by Balfour Beatty, the depot was handed over to South Yorkshire Supertram in July 1993. It consists of a three-road workshop, paint shop, six stabling sidings, a turning loop and engineers' siding. A staff halt was provided alongside the depot on the Meadowhall line; however, this later opened to the public as Nunnery Square to serve the adjacent Park & Ride.

Within the workshop there are two through lines, lines 8 and 9. Line 10, which is furthest away from the railway, is a bay that can

Above: On 23 February 1992 Class 37 No. 37144 heads an engineering train past the Nunnery depot site. At this point the frame of the workshop has already been erected, but it would be almost another 18 months until the completed depot was handed over to Supertram. **Paul Jackson**

only be accessed from the eastern end of the building. Only part of this is electrified. All three roads are equipped with inspection pits. A Hegenscheidt wheel lathe, capable of turning tram wheels in situ, is located in the middle of line 8. Its central position enables the doors at either end of the shed to be closed during wheel skimming. The east end of line 8 and the west end of line 10 serve as jacking areas

Left: 1005 passes Nunnery depot on 23 October 1993. The depot access road can be seen to the right of the tram, whilst the staff halt can be made out in the distance. **Paul Jackson**

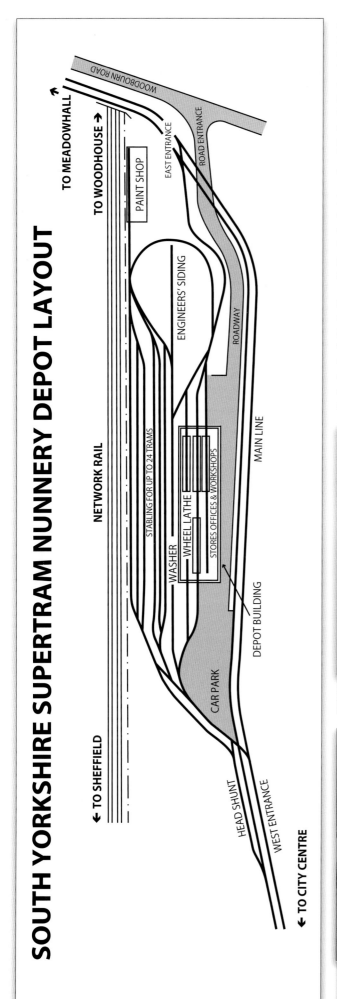

SOUTH YORKSHIRE SUPERTRAM NUNNERY DEPOT LAYOUT

TO MEADOWHALL

TO WOODHOUSE →

WOODBOURN ROAD

PAINT SHOP

EAST ENTRANCE

ROAD ENTRANCE

ENGINEERS' SIDING

NETWORK RAIL

ROADWAY

← TO SHEFFIELD

STABLING FOR UP TO 24 TRAMS

MAIN LINE

WASHER

WHEEL LATHE

STORES OFFICES & WORKSHOPS

DEPOT BUILDING

CAR PARK

HEAD SHUNT

WEST ENTRANCE

← TO CITY CENTRE

so that bogies can be removed from trams. Once removed, bogies can be moved onto the other shed roads by means of turntables at the west end of the building. They can then either be repaired or taken away by road transport, being lifted onto road vehicles using the six-tonne travelling crane that is installed above line 10. Smaller monohoists are also fitted above lines 9 and 10 and may be used in conjunction with the crane to facilitate multi-functional operations. A high-level platform between lines 9 and 10 enables staff to access the rooftop equipment and pantographs for servicing. Sanding apparatus, fed from a hopper on the north side of the building adjacent to line 7, is installed beside the two lines on the southern side of the shed.

The Nunnery substation, which provides power to part of the Meadowhall line and also the depot itself, is located in the south-west corner of the building. Two 600 kVA transformer rectifiers feed the tramway overhead, whilst a single 800 kVA transformer provides domestic supplies (415/240/110 V AC) to the depot. The substation is separated from a small general purpose workshop along the south side of the building by the internal stores.

At first floor level against the south wall there are the main offices, as well as the amenity and welfare facilities. The operation and power controller's office, the nerve centre of the system, from which operation is monitored using SCADA, CCTV and radio contact, has a panoramic view of the western depot approach. Also referred to as the Operations Control Centre, this room is supervised on a duty basis by two members of staff, one taking responsibility for communicating with tram drivers and monitoring tram activity via the automated vehicle location software, and the other overseeing the network's traction power and other

Above: The Hegenscheidt wheel lathe, which is located in the centre of line 8, on the northern side of the depot building. **Robert Pritchard**

Above: A rare view of the underside of a Supertram, as seen from one of the inspection pits. Note the magnetic track brakes between the wheels. **Ian Beardsley**

Left: The western end of line 10 is used as a jacking area. During the 25 October 2015 depot open day 118-2 and part of its articulation unit are seen here on stands. **Robert Pritchard**

Above: Supertrams 119 and 102 stand inside the main depot building on 10 December 2015. Alongside, on the left, is tram-train 399 201, which was about to be launched to the press. **Robert Pritchard**

Left: 103 and 124 occupy the east ends of lines 9 and 10 on 25 October 2015. A high-level platform between these lines allows engineering staff access to service pantographs and other rooftop equipment. **Robert Pritchard**

STRANGERS IN THE CAMP

Above: Supertram's Chief Executive and Engineering Manager thought it a good idea for the system to have a small diesel shunting loco to rescue any failed trams. With this in mind preserved BR Class 02 D2854 briefly visited the depot from its base at the South Yorkshire Railway near Meadowhall; however, the project was later abandoned and it is understood that the loco was never used. Here the loco is found standing at the eastern end of the depot site, where the Paint Shop is now located, on 16 November 1994. **Paul Jackson**

Right: Newly delivered ex-Berlin Reko Type TE64 works car 721 039-4, purchased for the princely sum of one Deutschmark, is pictured in Nunnery depot yard on 7 November 1996. Built in 1968 and originally numbered 5104, the vehicle was converted to a works car in 1980. Supertram acquired it with the intention of using it for rail grinding work and expected it to be available for duty by the beginning of 1998 following the replacement of its couplers, the fitting of a new Brecknell-Willis pantograph (the old one would not extend high enough in some locations on the Supertram network) and the installation of electronic equipment to operate the route-setting software. Although it made at least one trip into the city centre in the dead of night, it was very rarely seen outside of the depot confines and spent much of its time in the siding where the Paint Shop is now located, eventually being declared as surplus to requirements. It was then sold to the Tramway Museum Society as a source of spares for its ex-Berlin access tram 3006 and was moved to the TMS's Clay Cross stores building on 3 June 2000. From here it then moved to the National Tramway Museum, Crich on 14 February 2004 and was subsequently dismantled. **Paul Jackson**

Right: 114 and 117 are stabled in the depot yard on 25 October 2015, whilst 112 is about to go through the wash. **Robert Pritchard**

Left: A dedicated paint facility was constructed on the eastern side of the depot site in the late 1990s, replacing a paint booth at the western end of the main depot. Here we see 107, the first tram to be painted in the then new Stagecoach white livery, inside the Paint Shop on 5 May 1998. **Paul Jackson**

Below: The east end of the depot building, as viewed on 10 December 2015. Tram-train 399 201 is standing on road 10. **Robert Pritchard**

Below: The control staff's diagram of the network as it was in February 1998. Automated vehicle location software is used to monitor tram activity, including their location and what service they are on. A second computer in the Operations Control Centre is used to control traction power and other electrical supplies on the network. **Paul Jackson**

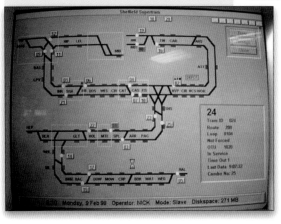

Left: A member of staff explains operations within the control centre to an audience of Branch Line Society members on 26 July 2009. The screen on the left shows the location of trams around the network, whilst that on the right displays the power controller's diagram. **Ian Beardsley**

electrical supplies through SCADA. If for any reason trams are not automatically recognised at road junctions, the controllers can also use a terminal to add a tram phase into the traffic light cycles around the city.

An automated wash plant is located on road 7 on the north side of the workshop. Up to 24 trams may be stabled outside on roads 1–6.

Trams can move on and off depot via connections at both ends. A double-track connection is provided at the west end, which also doubles as a headshunt to allow shunting to take place without tram movements having to interrupt operations on the main line. A steep single-track connection links the depot to the main running line alongside Woodbourn Road.

TRAM STOPS

Once the network was fully open there was a total of 45 tram stops, plus the staff halt adjacent to Nunnery depot. In the intervening years there have been several new stops opened and also one closure. The first of these additions came on 12 May 1997 when the staff halt was opened to the public as part of the Nunnery Square Park & Ride. Built in connection with the neighbouring leisure and entertainment complex, Valley Centertainment opened on 5 November the following year. A limited amount of car parking is also provided here for tram users. It would be another three years

before the next new stop, with Park Grange Croft opening on 21 December 2001. Then, on 27 October 2002, the Sheffield Station/ Sheffield Hallam University stop was resited slightly to the south as part of a £30 million investment in the station infrastructure by Midland Mainline, which was at that point the station operator. Also involving the relocation of the taxi rank to provide a much larger, brighter concourse, this project saw the installation of a new pedestrian footbridge to provide a direct link between the tram stop and the station platforms. Passengers previously had to cross to the eastern island platform (Platforms 6–8) and then use a separate bridge from here to access the tram stop. The original

Right: Since the completion of the Supertram network, several new tram stops have been opened around the network. On 11 November 2001 work is under way at Park Grange Croft. **Paul Jackson**

Below: On 7 April 2019 XPO Logistics-liveried 116 reverses at one of the original inbound platforms at Sheffield Station prior to forming a Blue Route service to Halfway. In the background 118, carrying adverts for PrettyLittleThing.com, stands between the other two original platforms. Supertram services on this date were partially suspended due to engineering works between Sheffield Station and Fitzalan Square. **Alan Yearsley**

Above: 113 calls at Meadowhall South/Tinsley on 4 August 2019. Most stops feature a standard design with platforms either side of the running line, equipped with basic platform furniture such as lights and waiting shelters. With relatively short waiting times elaborated stops were considered inappropriate, but in more recent times stops have had seating and real-time information displays installed. **Ian Beardsley**

stop was closed but its platforms remain in situ and can be used in the event of any service disruption.

A standard design, incorporating the recommendations of the Cranfield Institute, which SYPTE commissioned to study platform ergonomics for both able bodied and mobility impaired passengers, is used on all Supertram stops to help make them easy to understand and use. Platforms are typically 26½ m long and three metres wide, with a 1:20 slope at either end. To facilitate level access on and off the trams, the platforms are elevated 375 mm above rail level. A 600 mm-wide, light coloured, textured paving strip is installed at the edge of the platforms, with a 400 mm-wide tactile warning strip to its rear. Tactile paving is also provided across the width of the platforms to coincide with tram door locations. Supertram was the first UK system to feature tactile paving to assist blind or partially-sighted passengers.

Basic platform furniture, comprising Abacus waiting shelters, ticket vending machines and validators, lighting, signage and fencing, was provided at most stops upon the opening of the system and was designed to provide a quality image. After only a couple of years the ticket machines and validators were removed in favour of having on-board conductors. It was said at the time that the ticket machines were slow in operation and prone to vandalism. Few changes have since taken place. Passenger Information Displays, providing

Above: Another feature pioneered by Supertram was the use of tactile paving at tram stops to help blind or partially sighted passengers know where the edge of the platforms is and where the tram doors will be, seen here at Donetsk Way on the Halfway line. **Ian Beardsley**

real-time running information, have been operational at most tram stops since July 2015 and seating was installed at roughly half of the tram stops during upgrade work in early 2017.

In addition to those at Nunnery Square and Valley Centertainment, Park & Ride sites of varying sizes are provided at Carbrook Ikea, Halfway, Malin Bridge, Meadowhall and Middlewood. Where there is a charge for parking, for example at Halfway, ticket machines are provided for users to purchase combined tram and parking tickets.

A qualitative regime agreed between Stagecoach and the PTE ensures that all facilities are kept to a high standard. Supertram staff undertake annual paint programmes and vegetation management, as well as regular cleaning and inspections.

113 is pictured at White Lane on 31 July 2006 en route to Malin Bridge. Traffic islands are installed in the centre of the carriageway to prevent other road users from attempting to overtake trams whilst they are at stops. **Paul Jackson**

Right: 399 207 pauses at Halfway on 18 September 2019 prior to working an early evening service to Malin Bridge. To the right is one of the six Park & Ride car parks on the system, which with almost 200 spaces allows people from north-east Derbyshire and the south side of Sheffield to leave their cars and commute into Sheffield using public transport. On the left is a lay-by that allows people to be safely dropped off or picked up without disrupting traffic on the nearby roads; it is also the terminus of several bus routes. **Ian Beardsley**

TRACK
RENEWALS

By the early 2010s much of the existing tramway track was nearing life expiry, and in 2013 work started on the renewal of the track. When Supertram was at the planning stage the track was projected to last 30 years, although at this time it was envisaged that the trams would have only three bogies rather than four.

The new track is made of 330V high performance grooved rail developed by Tata Steel, which is made of harder-wearing steel and is thought to have a life expectancy of 25–30 years. It is designed to give high wear resistance and can be weld-repaired using Tata's patented weld process. The many tight curves on the Supertram network are liable to cause high levels of both vertical and side wear. Side wear can be restored repeatedly by welding: this involves a low pre-heat of 60–80°C, which avoids damage to the polymers surrounding the embedded rails and ensures the development of a tough steel microstructure that is resistant to cracking and produces robust, crack-free welds. The lifespan of the rail is thus determined solely by the amount of vertical wear.

Above: Track renewal in progress at Cathedral on 10 June 2015.
(**Inset:** A close-up of a section of rail.)
Robert Pritchard (2)

Left: Track welding being demonstrated by VolkerRail at the Nunnery depot open day on 25 October 2015. **Robert Pritchard**

Carbon content of the steel used for the rails is relatively high at 0.73–0.78%. The steel also contains 0.65–1% silicon, 1.1–1.4% manganese for hardenability, and 0.07–0.15% vanadium (which was first used in the chassis of the Ford Model T to increase the tenslie strength of the steel). The new rail has been developed by Tata metallurgists at the Swinden Technology Centre in Rotherham, working in conjunction with engineers at the rail mill in Hayange, France. An important design feature of the new track is that it has a profile with a deeper groove to cater for the different wheel profile of the tram-train vehicles.

Tram replacement buses were laid on to cover the routes closed for track renewal, including a mixture of non-stop and all-stops buses in some instances. Where an outer section of a route remained open some trams were usually outstationed to serve this section, although in some cases buses replaced trams over an entire section of the network even though work was only taking place on part of the route. No outstationing of trams took place in the second phase of work starting in 2018, however.

2013

The first phase of work, carried out by contractor VolkerRail, started on 30 June 2013 and involved the replacement of track on the crossing with Granville Road and the steep gradient and sharp curves of Park Grange Road. Herdings Park services were replaced by buses throughout, whilst Halfway trams ran only between Halfway and Spring Lane where passengers were transferred onto buses. On 16 September that year relaying work started on the crossover at Spring Lane, which had been used by terminating Halfway trams during the summer, necessitating the extension of replacement bus services to Gleadless Townend. This also enabled the track to be replaced on Ridgeway Road between Manor Top and Gleadless Townend.

2014

Full service on the Halfway and Herdings Park routes resumed on 4 November 2013, then on 29 March 2014 work started on the Middlewood and Malin Bridge line between Infirmary Road and Hillsborough. The Middlewood line reopened on 20 April and the Malin Bridge branch on 22 April, and further work took place between White Lane and Halfway from late April until mid-May. All lines were kept open for the Tour de France cycle race, which started in Leeds in 2014 and passed through Sheffield on 6 July that year. Track replacement work resumed after the Tour de France, this time centred on West Street in the city centre with buses replacing trams between Cathedral and the Malin Bridge and Middlewood termini. This work was completed in mid-September, but just before the end of this phase of work there was further disruption when a sink hole appeared by the Park Square triangle between Sheffield Station and Fitzalan Square on 31 August. Having already been curtailed at Cathedral, services on the Halfway and Herdings Park routes were further cut back to start and terminate at Sheffield Station. Trams on the Meadowhall line were still able to run to and from Cathedral. Full service on all lines resumed on 13 September.

2015

The first phase of works in 2015 took place from 28 March until 8 May between Infirmary Road and Hillsborough, with Blue Route trams running between Halfway and Shalesmoor and Yellow Route trams between Meadowhall and Cathedral. Replacement buses ran Shalesmoor–Malin Bridge and Cathedral–Middlewood (non-stop between Cathedral and Shalesmoor).

Above: Track renewal in progress at Manor Top on 6 July 2013. **Paul Jackson**

During the first phase of track renewals in the summer of 2013, the conductor of car 123 changes the points on the crossover at Gleadless Townend with a point iron to enable the tram to reverse and form a service to Halfway on 6 July that year. **Paul Jackson**

This was followed by work in the Fitzalan Square area from 11 May to 1 June, when direct services ran to Meadowhall from Halfway and Herdings Park. These used the part of Park Square triangle that is only normally used for empty workings to and from Nunnery depot. Trams to and from Malin Bridge and Middlewood started and terminated at Castle Square, with a replacement bus service operating on a circular route: Cathedral–Sheffield Station–Granville Road–Fitzalan Square–Cathedral. Alternatively passengers could walk between Cathedral or Castle Square and Sheffield Station.

Then on 2 June the work moved to the section between Cathedral and Castle Square, resulting in the two main routes being split in two: Halfway–Fitzalan Square and Shalesmoor–Malin Bridge (Blue Route) and Meadowhall–Fitzalan Square and University–Middlewood (Yellow Route). Purple Route trams ran only between Herdings Park and Sheffield Station. Two replacement bus routes ran between Fitzalan Square and Shalesmoor: one non-stop and one serving all stops. Full service resumed on 27 June, then from 29 June until 28 August further track replacement work took place on Ridgeway Road, which required a closure between Sheffield Station and Gleadless Townend. Blue Route services ran Malin Bridge–Sheffield Station and Gleadless Townend–Halfway with the Purple Route suspended completely. Yellow Route trams were unaffected. Two replacement bus routes were provided: one limited stop between Fitzalan Square and Gleadless Townend calling only at Manor Top, and one between Fitzalan Square and Herdings Park serving all stops. This was the final phase of track replacement work until 2018.

2018

In 2018 VolkerRail was again awarded the contract for the next phase of renewal works, which is expected to continue until 2024. The first stage of this started on 26 May and continued until 15 June, involving replacement of the trackwork at the entrance to Middlewood Park

& Ride site, the Middlewood diamond, Catch Bar Lane and adjacent to Hillsborough Park Bowling Club on Middlewood Road. The next phase of work took place in the Birley Lane, Birley Moor Road, Sheffield Road and Donetsk Way areas on the Halfway line from 23 June to 11 August (additional finishing works delaying completion of this phase from the originally planned date of 8 August) and on Norton Avenue on the Herdings Park branch on 10–19 August. Then from 25 August until 9 September it was the turn of the pointwork at Gleadless Townend to receive attention, meaning that buses replaced trams from there to Halfway and Herdings Park. Finally from 10 to 16 September the Halfway branch was closed between Donetsk Way and Halfway for track work near Eckington Way between Beighton Drake House Lane and Halfway.

2019

Further works took place at Hillsborough Corner and along Middlewood Road from 19 April to 2 June 2019, closing the lines between Hillsborough Interchange and Malin Bridge (Blue Route) and Middlewood (Yellow Route). This was followed by Shalesmoor–Hillsborough from 3 June to 18 July. All lines remained open for the annual Tramlines music festival in Hillsborough Park, then the Hillsborough Corner and Holme Lane area saw further track renewals from 27 July to 3 August and 18–23 August, likewise closing the Malin Bridge and Middlewood branches beyond Hillsborough. A normal service ran from 5 to 16 August and until about 21.00 on 17 August, and on 4 August work took place only on Holme Lane so Middlewood trams could still run. The final phase of work for 2019 took place on Glossop Road between Cathedral and University from 24 to 30 August, with all lines closed west of Cathedral. A replacement bus service ran between the city centre and Malin Bridge, and Supertram Link route SL1, which normally runs between Middlewood and Stocksbridge, was extended to and from Fitzalan Square via Shalesmoor.

Track renewal in progress at Park Grange on 5 July 2013. **Paul Jackson**

Right: Track renewal in progress on Park Square Bridge on 11 May 2015. **Paul Jackson**

THE
TRAM FLEET

The original Supertram fleet consists of 25 three-section trams built by Siemens-Duewag in Düsseldorf, Germany, numbered 101–125 (originally 01–25). Siemens was awarded the contract to build the trams on 13 December 1990 and construction started during the second half of 1992. Several of the trams underwent trial runs on the Rheinbahn network in Düsseldorf during the summer of 1993 before being shipped to the UK. The first training phase for drivers and driving instructors also took place in Germany. Cars 01, 02 and 03 were delivered from Germany with the numbers "1001", "1002" and "1003" applied on the cab fronts, but they never carried these in passenger service. These numbers were those allocated by the Rheinbahn for use when on trials on its system.

Car 02 was the first to be delivered to Sheffield on 26 August 1993. This car, along with the others, was transported on low loaders via the Rotterdam–Immingham ferry and then by road to Nunnery depot. Table 2 shows the delivery dates for the 25 trams, along with the first date that each was seen operating under its own power outside of the depot confines. The cars themselves are owned by South Yorkshire Light Rail Ltd, a subsidiary of the South Yorkshire Passenger Transport Executive (SYPTE).

TECHNICAL DETAILS

Sheffield's Siemens-Duewag trams are widely acknowledged to be the best trams on any of the modern UK light rail systems – with comfortable seats and excellent riding

Above: The frame is laid for the first of the new trams for Sheffield in the Duewag Works in Düsseldorf. Duewag became part of Siemens in 1989. **Roger Jones/ South Yorkshire Supertram Ltd**

qualities on both on-street and segregated track. The trams are double-articulated three-section cars with four motored bogies, two of which are located under the ends of the central body section. Official Siemens literature refers to the two end sections as A and B, and the centre section, which is joined to these by means of two articulations, as C. The driving cars have, however, been numbered by Supertram as xx-1 and xx-2, with the centre section being xx-3. The pantograph is mounted on the centre section.

Above: The first tram takes shape in Düsseldorf. **Roger Jones/South Yorkshire Supertram Ltd**

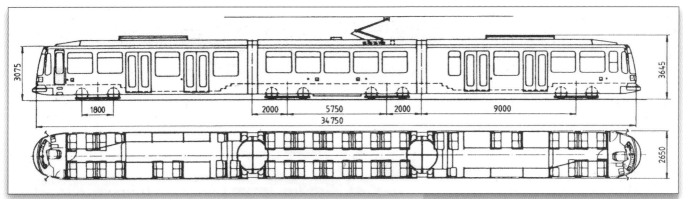

Above: The original drawings of the three-section articulated tram for Sheffield. **Courtesy Siemens**

Left: This South Yorkshire Supertram model was displayed in the window of Sheffield's Marks & Spencer in December 1990, providing an interesting comparison with the how the real thing turned out. **Paul Jackson**

Right: The first tram for Sheffield, 1002, leaves the Duewag Works on the start of its journey to South Yorkshire in August 1993. **Roger Jones/South Yorkshire Supertram Ltd**

Below: In this undated view taken in summer 1993 pioneer car 1001 (later 01 and then 101) is seen alongside Rheinbahn Type B80 car 4269 at Düsseldorf Hoterheide station whilst on an early commissioning trial. Car 01 was actually the seventh car to be delivered to Sheffield, after 02–07. **Roger Jones/South Yorkshire Supertram Ltd**

TABLE I. SIEMENS-DUEWAG SUPERTRAM FLEET (AFTER REFURBISHMENT)

Built	1992–94 by Siemens-Duewag, Düsseldorf, Germany.
Wheel arrangement	B-B-B-B.
Traction motors	4 x monomotor drives of 265 kW (355 hp).
Line voltage	750 V DC.
Track gauge	1435 mm.
Seats	80 (+6).
Standing capacity	155 standing at 4 pass/m², 232 standing at 6 pass/m².
Weight	52 tonnes.
Braking	Regenerative, disc & emergency track brakes.
Wheel diameter	670 mm (new); 590 mm (worn).
Couplers	Albert (emergency use).
Maximum speed	50 mph (80 km/h).
Doors	Sliding plug.
Auxiliary voltage	24 V DC.
Dimensions:	
Length	34.75 m.
Width	2.65 m.
Height	3.64 m.
Performance data:	
Max acceleration	1.3 m/s².
Max deceleration (service brake)	1.5 m/s².
Max deceleration (emergency brakes)	3 m/s².

Below: 26 August 1993 was an historic day in the Supertram project, with the first tram, 1002 (later 02) arriving from Germany. It is seen here on the final leg of its journey to Nunnery depot. **Paul Jackson**

The trams are 34.75 m long: at the time they were built they were one of the longest articulated trams – only the articulated DT8 type for the Stuttgart light rail system and the GT8-100 articulated cars for Karlsruhe were longer. The long trams arose from the desire to ensure that a single tram could handle the maximum amount of traffic – cars wouldn't need to operate in multiple, which wasn't seen as desirable. Since the Supertrams of the early 1990s, much longer trams have been constructed for other systems, such as Budapest and Dublin, where trams of 55 m length are now in service.

Because the Sheffield system has gradients as steep as 10% (1 in 10) it was necessary for all axles to be powered, effectively limiting the low-floor area to that between the bogies. Two bogies are located beneath the centre section and one beneath the outer end of each driving section with a wheelbase of 1800 mm. All bogies are interchangeable, except that the outer bogies of four trams were supplied with flange lubricators to reduce wheel wear. The tram body is supported on the bogies via ball-bearing ring races. The bogie bolster has a secondary air-bag suspension system that is designed to cope with the transverse forces that occur on trams. The air-suspension system is supplemented by elastomer stops that can support the tram body should the air bags become deflated. The primary system for axle suspension uses rubber chevrons. The bogie frame is of a hollow box-girder design. The load-bearing elements and welds are designed to ensure that the bogie frame can cope with all the stresses of street operation. The shock-absorbers for vertical and transverse forces operate hydraulically. The tram wheels have Bochum type-84 resilient rubber insets and have a diameter of 670 mm when new to 590 mm when fully worn.

The car body is of Corten-B steel in welded construction. The outer skin provides the frame with additional strength. Maximum clearance and optimum safety is provided at the articulations, and this is achieved by the passageways having the same high quality for the inside skin as for the main body sections. Special rubber seals were used to prevent any dirt entering the tram via the articulation skins. All of the external surfaces were primed and painted, and the inside sections specially primed to provide protection against corrosion. A layer of sound-damping material was also fitted.

Above: The first time an electric tram had been seen on the streets of Sheffield since 1960 – the first tram delivered to Sheffield, 1002 (later 02 and then 102) is seen crossing Woodbourn Road on its first test run on 17 September 1993 – this was a gauging run from the depot to Meadowhall. The tram is displaying "Sonderzug" on its blind – German for "Special Train", although it is doubtful that many local residents would have known what it meant! **Peter Fox**

The four traction motors are air-cooled DC monomotors of type 1KB2121 with a one hour rating of around 265 kW controlled by GTO (Gate Turn-Off) semi-conductors. It was possible to dispense with braking series resistors as a result of a suitable motor design, and this brought energy savings through regenerative braking.

The disc brakes are of the German Federspeicherbramse type (translated as "Spring-loaded brake"), they are spring applied and air-released, with each axle having one disc brake. The electric brake is sufficient to require blended air+electric braking during service braking. The air brake can be used as a replacement service brake should the electric brake fail on either traction control unit, to take over braking gradually at speeds below 12 km/h, and as a parking brake. Each half of the car has its own traction control unit, so if the brake should fail on one, air braking takes over for that half of the vehicle. The air supply is provided by a compressor, driven by a 380-volt 100 Hz three-phase motor, with the unit installed below the floor. The brake cylinders are

Below: On its gauging run from Nunnery to Meadowhall, 1002 stops near Arena on 17 September 1993. **Paul Jackson**

TABLE 2: SIEMENS-DUEWAG FLEET DELIVERY DATES

Tram No.	Date delivered to Nunnery depot	Date first observed running
01	3 November 1993	13 November 1993
02	26 August 1993	17 September 1993
03	29 September 1993	16 May 1994
04	8 September 1993	20 September 1993
05	23 September 1993	23 October 1993
06	13 October 1993	21 July 1994
07	27 October 1993	26 November 1993
08	19 November 1993	2 December 1993
09	26 November 1993	6 January 1994
10	8 December 1993	7 January 1994
11	21 December 1993	20 January 1994
12	13 January 1994	18 February 1994
13	26 January 1994	21 March 1994
14	9 February 1994	22 March 1994
15	24 February 1994	18 March 1994
16	8 March 1994	8 July 1994
17	21 March 1994	30 June 1994
18	6 April 1994	21 July 1994
19	20 April 1994	21 July 1994
20	3 May 1994	21 July 1994
21	17 May 1994	21 July 1994
22	9 June 1994	29 July 1994
23	15 June 1994	29 July 1994
24	6 July 1994	2 September 1994
25	21 July 1994	2 September 1994

Notes:

Nos. 01–03 were delivered from Germany as 1001–1003. For a brief time some other vehicles carried 10xx series numbers on card panels in the cab fronts.

Date first observed running refers to when trams were first seen operating outside the confines of Nunnery depot. In some cases these will refer to trams on test running or driver training, whilst others went straight into passenger-carrying service.

of the stored spring type – the braking force acts on the disc when the air pressure falls. All of the brake cylinders have an automatic adjusting device to ensure that there is a constant clearance between the brake block and disc irrespective of the degree of block wear. The brake cylinders also have a manual mechanical release accessible from outside the tram. In addition they have a release through an auxiliary air system to enable recovery in the event of failure. Each bogie has two magnetic track brake magnets for emergency use, each with a contact force of 50 kN and these can give a deceleration of 3 m/s^2.

There are concealed emergency Albert couplers at each end of the tram for emergency rescue purposes. The air-operated swing-plug doors open outwards and provide an opening of 1.3 m wide and 2.045 m high.

The trams are double-ended and the driving cabs have glazed partitions to give the driver good visibility back down the car and also passengers sitting in the front seats a good view forward (although drivers can also pull down a blind to restrict the forward view). The driving seat and controls were arranged ergonomically. The cab extends across the whole width of the tram and the driver can leave either via their own side door or via a door into the passenger area in the middle of the bulkhead. The driving seat is centrally positioned, with a tip-up seat provided next to the driving seat for an assistant or supervisor.

In an emergency buttons on the passenger grab bars enable two-way communication between the driver and a passenger. Microphones in the PA system also allow the driver to monitor what is happening in the passenger compartment. From the cab, each vehicle also has direct contact with the control centre.

INTERIOR SPECIFICATION

A total of 40% of the length of each tram is classed as "low-floor". All four entrance doors on each side are in the two driving sections and are at a height of 420 mm, which matches the height of the platforms at each tram stop, thus ensuring level access. There is then, in the low-floor section, a gentle slope up to a height of 480 mm, where there are tip-up seats, priority seats, and space for pushchairs and wheelchairs. By not having any doors in the centre section it was possible to have a continuous floor height of 880 mm in this high-floor section, so that both axles of one bogie can be driven from a single longitudinal motor. The high-floor section is reached via three steps and the high-floor section behind each cab (also at 880 mm) is reached via two steps. There are therefore three distinct sections in each tram:

- The two end sections: These adjoin the driving cabs with 15 seats accessible via two fairly steep steps, seen as suitable for passengers on medium-length journeys;
- The two sections by the four doorways (one in each end section): These have limited seating (ten seats each) but with space for wheelchairs, mobility scooters and prams etc at entry level, seen as best suited to passengers on shorter journeys or for standing passengers at peak times;
- The centre section: This has the most seating, a total of 40 seats arranged in facing "bays of four" and reached via three steps from the entrances, seen as suitable for passengers on medium or longer distance journeys.

Left: 1002 is seen on the approach to Meadowhall, as a Class 142 passes on the main line, again on 17 September 1993. **Paul Jackson**

Right: The second tram to be delivered was 04 on 8 September 1993, seen here completing the last part of its journey to Nunnery depot during heavy rain. **Paul Jackson**

On the first gauging test run into the city centre, 04 is seen at Fitzalan Square on 5 November 1993. **Paul Jackson**

Therefore, in as-built condition the trams had 88 seats. Almost all seats are arranged in 2+2 facing bays, except that the priority seats at the inner end of each driving section are unidirectional and 2+1. There are two pairs of seats close to the articulation at the top of the steps to the centre section (opposite the equipment cabinet on the other side of the aisle). As-built there were no tip-up seats, although it had been originally planned to have four tip-up seats in the area instead reserved for wheelchairs and prams. The seats themselves (almost all double seats secured on frames) are the same type as used on the Duewag trams in Stuttgart.

The interior was designed to meet stringent safety requirements and interior fittings are free from sharp edges that could injure passengers in the event of the tram stopping quickly. Particular attention was paid to the provision of grab rails and strap hangers, which hang from most of the horizontal grab rails. Two enclosed equipment cubicles replace what would have been single seats. These house the electronic control system, offering easy access for maintenance. Otherwise the electrical equipment is distributed under the floor of the centre section, with traction control equipment located on the roof of the end sections.

REFURBISHMENT

A major £2 million refurbishment programme started in late 2005, with car 115 the first to be dealt with. 115 was launched to the media at Nunnery depot on 27 January 2006 sporting a striking new livery of mainly blue with red and orange "swooshes" at the ends. Work on each tram took around seven weeks to complete, and the programme was finished with car 116 outshopped on 23 January 2009.

As part of the refurbishment programme the number of seats was reduced to 80 conventional and six tip-up seats (three in each end section). The number of wheelchair spaces remained unchanged, but to comply with disabled access regulations this facility is now on the opposite side of the aisle and has a larger bulkhead either side than

Above: Traction control equipment is located on the roof of the end sections. 120, before its cab air-conditioning "pod" was fitted, is seen heading down Park Grange Road towards the city centre and Malin Bridge on 22 April 2011. **Ian Beardsley**

previously. One bay of four facing seats was removed and this is now the area where one wheelchair can be accommodated, with three tip-up seats in the former wheelchair area opposite.

Refurbishment also involved the replacement of the original pale blue seat moquette with the corporate Stagecoach darker blue, fitting of yellow instead of green interior grab poles for better visibility, replacement of manual announcements by the driver with pre-recorded voices announcing the name of each stop, and fitting separate buttons to open the doors and request the driver to stop at the next stop (previously the same button was used for both functions). The lighting was also enhanced, being brighter and with new diffusers, and new flooring was fitted. More recently trams have started to be fitted with a slightly updated version of the blue upholstery like that used in the new Stadler trams.

Just prior to the start of the refurbishment programme, the cars started to be fitted with digital destination displays to replace the manually operated destination roller-blinds previously used. Car 105 was the first to be so equipped in early 2005. Destination displays were also installed on the sides as well as at the cab ends for the first time. Destinations are still occasionally displayed using manual destination indicators in the lower cab front in the event of the digital destination displays failing.

Right: A view of tram 118 split at Nunnery depot on 25 October 2015, showing the articulation between the end section and the centre section. **Robert Pritchard**

Left: In summer 2011 experimental cab air-conditioning pods were fitted to car 110 and this later led to the fleet-wide fitting of similar equipment. 110 is seen on 17 August 2011 on High Street heading to Middlewood. **Paul Jackson**

Below: A broadside view of 105 approaching Meadowhall on 6 December 2008 shows the three separate sections, with the pantograph raised on the middle, high-floor, section. **Robert Pritchard**

Above: A few weeks after being outshopped in the then new Stagecoach mainly white livery, 107 arrives at Hollinsend with a Blue Route service to Halfway on 30 May 1998. **Paul Jackson**

Below: Showing the revised version of the original Stagecoach livery, with a dark blue lower bodyside stripe, 125 leaves Cathedral on 20 August 2001. **Paul Jackson**

Above: The first tram to receive an advertising livery was 120 in Ask JON colours in 1999. Shortly after it received the vinyl wrap it stands at Cathedral on 1 December 1999. **Paul Jackson**

Left: In March 2004 the centre section of 110 received a special livery promoting ten years of Supertram. The message along the top reads "Stagecoach Supertram – A Splendid Service". The tram is seen on 31 March 2004 at Gleadless Townend. **Paul Jackson**

Right: A close up of the purple Meadowhall livery on 116, pictured at Castle Square on 2 September 2008. **Robert Pritchard**

Apart from these, and the various livery changes over the years (see below), the only other significant modification to have been carried out on the fleet is the fitting of new air conditioning to the cabs. Experimental roof-mounted air conditioning "pods" or boxes were fitted to car 110 in the summer of 2011, and subsequently a slightly different, squarer, design of pod has been fitted to every tram at both ends (110 retains its non-standard pods). Some of the pods have now been painted red, instead of the original white or light grey, to better fit with the fleet livery, although those on 120 have been left grey to match its livery. The passenger saloon is not air-conditioned but has opening windows and a high-capacity ventilation and heating system.

LIVERIES

The original livery was a rather uninspiring plain pale grey with a dark grey base. Following Stagecoach being awarded the operating franchise in 1997 the entire fleet was painted into a version of that company's then corporate livery, consisting of white with orange, red and medium blue stripes at the bottom. The first car to be outshopped in the mainly white livery (107) was released on 5 May 1998. As cars were repainted they were renumbered by the addition of 100 to their number, so 01 became 101 and so on. All trams had been repainted in the mainly white livery by 2000; however, the livery was later revised with the addition of a dark blue stripe on the lower bodyside.

At the same time as the vehicles were refurbished (between 2006 and 2009), the white livery was replaced by the present day mainly dark blue livery with red cab ends and an orange "swoosh" just behind each cab end. The doors are also orange to comply with disabled access regulations, which require the doors to be of a different colour to the main body of the vehicle to improve visibility for partially-sighted passengers. This livery more closely represented the livery that Stagecoach used

TABLE 3: ADVERTISING AND SPECIAL LIVERIES CARRIED

Tram No.	Livery	Year Applied
104	My Sheffield Jobs orange	2007
106	Thomson Fly pale blue	2006
109	East Midlands Trains pink	2019
110	Supertram 10th anniversary blue (centre section only)	2004
111	East Midlands Trains blue	2010
	IKEA pale blue	2017
	Pretty Little Thing pink	2018*
116	Meadowhall blue	2004
	Meadowhall purple	2006
	Genting Club casino black/red	2012
	East Midlands Trains blue	2014
	Doncaster Sheffield Airport purple/red/turquoise	2017
	XPO Logistics red/white	2019*
118	Pretty Little Thing pink	2018*
120	Ask JON green	1999
	Meadowhall (light blue on one side, pink on the other)	2001
	East Midlands Trains blue	2009
	Pseudo Sheffield Corporation cream/blue	2010*

Note: * Still carried in early 2020.

In the colourful advertising livery for the My Sheffield Jobs website, 104 descends Park Grange Road, between the Spring Lane and Arbourthorne Road stops, with a Blue Route service for Malin Bridge on 7 February 2009. **Robert Pritchard**

on many of its trains, including those operated by South West Trains and East Midlands Trains. Some trams have now carried the Stagecoach blue livery longer than the other liveries put together, and already some have been repainted into blue a second time. This livery is expected to continued to be carried as standard, at least until the end of the current Stagecoach concession in 2024.

ADVERTISEMENT AND NON-STANDARD LIVERIES

Several of the trams have carried various advertising liveries and other non-standard colour schemes over the years. In most cases these were only carried for a fairly short period (usually no more than a year or two) before being replaced by another advertising livery or reverting to the Stagecoach corporate colour scheme. The first tram to receive an advertising livery was 120 in November 1999, which received dark green vinyls promoting the Ask JON telephone service (JON standing for Just One Number). The livery also controversially included "contravision" vinyls across the windows. As Meadowhall

Above: In a fairly short-lived advertising livery for Thomson Fly, 106 stands at Cathedral with a Blue Route service for Halfway on 16 July 2007. **Paul Jackson**

shopping centre – one of the largest shopping centres in the country – is served by Supertram it came as no surprise when it wished to advertise on Supertram. Both trams 116 and 120 have carried adverts for Meadowhall over the years. In 2001 120 lost its Ask JON livery in favour of a Meadowhall livery that was unusual as it was different colours (turquoise blue and pink) on either side.

Car 120 went on to carry a number of special liveries, its most famous being the plain cream with blue doors livery it received in October 2010. This was applied to commemorate the 50th anniversary of the closure of Sheffield's first generation tramway in October 1960,

and was designed to be as close as possible to the Sheffield Corporation livery carried by the city's previous tram fleet in their last few years of operation. Initially 120 didn't carry front end numbers, but these were later reapplied: it was originally thought that 120 would only carry this livery for a number of months, but it still carries these colours to this day.

By contrast, car 109 carried a very short-lived East Midlands Trains promotional livery in 2019, but this was removed and replaced by the standard Stagecoach Supertram livery with the end of the old EMT franchise (also held by Stagecoach) and its replacement by East

Right: Car 116 carried the distinctive black and red livery for Genting Club between 2012 and 2014. Shortly after being outshopped in this scheme, on 20 August 2012 it is seen passing the disused platforms at Sheffield Station on its way to Malin Bridge. **Robert Pritchard**

Above: In East Midlands Trains blue livery, car 120 is seen on Infirmary Road, approaching the Langsett/Primrose View stop with a Yellow Route service for Middlewood on 31 January 2010. **Robert Pritchard**

Above: A few months after being outshopped in pseudo Sheffield Corporation livery, but at this stage without any external running numbers, 120 approaches Birley Lane on 2 March 2011. **Ian Beardsley**

Right: Inside car 120 are posters marking 50 years since the old Sheffield trams finished in 1960. **Paul Jackson**

Midlands Railway, operated by Netherlands Railways subsidiary Abellio.

In September 2017 car 111 received a light blue scheme for IKEA to mark the opening of the new IKEA store in Sheffield on 28 September that year. The IKEA store is located close to the Carbrook stop, which was subsequently renamed Carbrook IKEA. The interior received a temporary IKEA-style makeover with new white and blue seat covers, flooring and multi-coloured cutlery pictured on the ceiling!

As part of the 21st anniversary celebrations and an open day held at Nunnery depot on 25 October 2015 (which was a great success and attracted almost 2000 people), car 123 received vinyl "people pictures" in the windows depicting fictional passengers. These were drawn by local artist Pete McKee. One even depicts a dog even though these aren't allowed on Supertram (except for guide dogs).

Table 3 shows a summary of all such liveries to have been carried by the Supertram fleet, with the year in which each livery was first applied. A number of partial adverts (often at roof level) have also been carried by many cars.

Above: The short-lived IKEA-liveried tram, 111, leaves Cathedral with a Blue Route service to Malin Bridge on 15 September 2017. The lettering on the centre car reads "The Wonderful Everyday is coming IKEA Sheffield opens 28th September". **Paul Jackson**

Left: Interior of IKEA tram 111 showing the mainly white upholstery. **Alan Yearsley**

CURRENT OPERATIONS

The Supertram fleet has always been highly utilised, with timetables historically demanding 23 of the 25 trams in service on weekdays. The arrival of the seven new Stadler tram-trains, three of which were intended for use on the original system, has eased the pressure on the older trams somewhat, as they now require more maintenance as they pass their 25th birthday.

The current peak timetable sees three tram-trains required for service (see Tram-Train section) and 23 other trams. These 23 should be drawn from the pool of 25 original trams and three Stadler trams designed to be used on the original tramway (i.e. not to Rotherham). It is normally planned that 21 Siemens trams and two Stadler trams will be used on the core system. At peak times the Blue Route demands 12 trams (ten off-peak), the Yellow Route nine trams (eight off-peak) and the Purple Route two trams. An additional tram is usually kept available at the depot as a "hot spare". Therefore, including the hot spare, 27 out of the total fleet of 32 trams are currently diagrammed to work daily.

For those wishing to view the trams, all services pass through the Cathedral–Fitzalan Square section in the city centre, meaning that this is the best place for observing trams. The Cathedral stop can be regarded as the hub of the operation, with tram-trains and Purple Route trams terminating and reversing here, five times per hour. Around an hour and a half's observation here will pick up all trams in service, the Blue Route trams from Halfway taking the longest to repeat.

Above: The drawings on 123, launched at Nunnery depot as part of the family open day on 25 October 2015. **Robert Pritchard**

Below: Another short-lived livery was the East Midlands Trains pink scheme applied to 109. On 27 May 2019 109 pauses at Cathedral with a Blue Route service to Halfway. **Paul Jackson**

111 has carried three different advertising liveries. The latest, applied in 2018, is for the Pretty Little Thing ladies fashion website. The tram wears a light pink livery adorned with images of dancing unicorns! This livery is also carried by 118. On 25 October 2018 111 calls at Meadowhall South with a Yellow Route service to Middlewood. Note the poppy on the right-hand side, trams usually carry these for around two-to-three weeks before Remembrance Day each year. **Robert Pritchard**

The current livery displayed on 109 as it approaches Sheffield Station with a Blue Route service for Halfway on 29 August 2019. Note the old manual destination blind (stating "Cathedral") which can be seen on the left-hand side of the driver's cab – these are still used in the event of the digital display failing. **Robert Pritchard**

THE INTERIORS

Two views of the original interior, **Right** the high-floor centre section and **Below** the multi-function area around the doors. On refurbishment the four fixed seats and one wheelchair space were replaced by three tip-up seats opposite one wheelchair space. **Paul Jackson (2)**

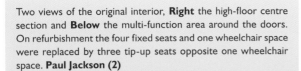

Below: Interior of the high-floor centre section of tram 112, refurbished with a pleasing deep blue upholstery and with yellow grab rails. **Robert Pritchard**

Above: Three tip-up seats now sit opposite the wheelchair space in each end section. These were fitted during the £2 million refurbishment programme started in late 2005. **Robert Pritchard**

Above left: There are two quite steep steps to access the seating area behind the driver's cab, seen here in car 125, and **Above right** three shallower steps from the end sections to access the centre section. Note that the seats left and right are marked as "priority seating", although the legroom in these seats is quite poor. The section above the articulation can be seen just beyond the steps. **Robert Pritchard (2)**

Right: The area around the two sets of doors in tram 112, looking towards the driver's cab and showing the dedicated wheelchair space (left) and tip-up seats (right). The request to stop buttons can also be seen (illuminated) on the left and right hand poles closest to the camera. **Robert Pritchard**

Left: A view of the driver's cab in tram 112 with the combined power/brake controller to the right of the driver. **Robert Pritchard**

ACCIDENTS

In the first 25 years of Supertram operation there have been a number of accidents, the most notable of which was undoubtedly on 25 October 2018 when 399 204 was derailed crossing Staniforth Road. This incident, and that on 30 November 2018 at the same location, are detailed in the Tram-Train section of this book. Here we concentrate solely on those accidents which resulted in some of Supertram's original Siemens-Duewag fleet being permanently misformed. Due to space limitations relatively minor derailments and other incidents are not featured.

The first such event occurred on 26 May 1995, before the system had even fully opened, with car 02 colliding with a Mainline bus on West Street. It was reported at the time that the bus had not pulled into a lay-by properly. Fortunately there were no serious injuries to passengers or staff, but the No. 1 end of 02 was badly damaged and had to be sent to ABB's Derby Carriage Works for repair, replaced by an end section of tram 11. On 22 June 1995 the latter had split a switch at Nunnery depot and damaged one its articulation units, the repairs to this necessitating it being taken out of service for a lengthy period. 11-1 was married with the undamaged sections of tram 02 in order to get one of the two back into traffic as quickly as possible, the reformed 02 returning to service on 14 July 1995. Tram 11 re-entered service in January the following year (with driving cars 11-2 and 02-1) but on 23 November 1996 it again split a pair of points, this time on the Meadowhall line alongside the M1 viaduct at Alsing Road.

Trams 118 and 120 have been similarly reformed following an incident at Shalesmoor on the morning of 22 October 2015. At the time (approximately 08.25) both trams were travelling towards the city centre, 118 on a Yellow Route service from Middlewood, and 120 on a late running Blue Route service from Malin Bridge. Being peak time, both trams were well loaded. 118 was standing at the Shalesmoor stop, its exit blocked by traffic queuing on the approach to Shalesmoor roundabout (despite there being a yellow box junction next to the tram stop here!). Tram 120 failed to stop and collided with the rear of 118 at a speed of approximately 8 mph. One member of staff and 15 passengers received minor injuries as a consequence of the collision; both trams were seriously damaged, however, and staff were unable to move 118 until around 05.00 the following morning. It was eventually towed back to Nunnery depot by 113. Prior to this the tram had to be split for engineering staff to inspect its articulation, damage to which had prevented it being moved the previous day. Tram 120 was driven wrong line to the emergency crossover at Hillsborough and then returned using the outbound line as far as the crossover just beyond Shalesmoor. Four other trams, which were similarly stranded, made the same manoeuvre, all under Police supervision during the early hours of 23 October 2015. Tram services to Malin Bridge and Middlewood, which in the aftermath

Above: The first major collision involving a Supertram left one of the driving cars of tram 02 (02-1) with a badly damaged front end, as seen in this view of it at Nunnery depot on 5 June 1995. **Paul Jackson**

Above: 11 is rerailed after splitting the points at Alsing Road on 23 November 1996. Note the damaged windscreen. **Paul Jackson**

Left: 02-1 is seen at Nunnery on 26 October 1995 following the fitting of a new/repaired cab front at ABB's Derby Carriage Works. **Paul Jackson**

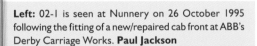

Right: On 1 December 2015 120's damaged driving car is seen out of use inside Nunnery depot. It is coupled to two vehicles from 118 (118-1 and 118-3). The ramp in the foreground has been assembled in preparation for the delivery of tram-train 399 201, the first of the seven Citylink vehicles to arrive at the depot. **Paul Jackson**

of the incident had been terminating at Netherthorpe Road and later in the outbound platform at Shalesmoor, returned to normal later this day. Owing to the shortage of trams Herdings Park–Meadowhall Purple Route services were truncated at Cathedral on Mondays–Saturdays from early that November, and in early December they were replaced by buses during the day.

Following a successful test run the day before, tram 120 re-entered service on 10 December 2015, with its damaged driving car (120-2) being replaced by 118-2, which had been repainted in matching cream and blue pseudo Sheffield Corporation livery. Its return to traffic allowed Supertram to reintroduce a full daytime service to the Herdings branch. The damaged sections of 118 were initially expected to be moved to a major works for repairs, but these were instead undertaken at Nunnery and 118 eventually returned to operation in early October 2016. Whilst out of traffic it also received a new interior trim in the same style as that used on the tram-trains.

In its report into the event the Rail Accident Investigation Board (RAIB) stated that tram 120 was not being driven in an appropriate manner considering the low railhead adhesion (caused by a combination of crushed leaves and morning dew) at the time. Its brakes therefore did not provide the level of braking that the driver, who had over 20 years' experience of driving Sheffield trams, expected. In normal circumstances the magnetic track brakes, which were deployed 25 m before the collision, would have brought 120 to a stand before it reached the preceding tram, but the higher than usual speed at which 120 had been travelling (it is presumed to make up time) and the poor adhesion combined meant that the "hazard brakes" were not sufficient to prevent the collision.

Maintenance of the tram and tramway infrastructure were not considered to have had an effect, but Stagecoach Supertram was criticised for its management of low railhead adhesion. Company procedures required it to reinforce awareness of low adhesion conditions through the publication of a "Winterisation Brief" which was to be issued by 1 October each year; this, however, was not supplied to staff until 28 October that year (after the event).

It was also found that tram drivers had not been correctly reporting all instances of wheel slide to the Operations Control Centre (OCC). In most cases the OCC was only made aware of low adhesion when this caused an indication to appear on the trams' in-cab vehicle status panel. The annunciator panel as it is known cannot, however, be relied upon to indicate all wheel slide events. The software controlling the system only informs the driver of a fault after a set threshold is exceeded and the system's counter is reset whenever the driver changes ends. In its report the RAIB said that drivers should have instead made reports to the OCC when sensing low deceleration or extended stopping distances and also when hearing the sanding gear, which is automatically triggered by the trams' wheel slide protection system, in operation. The OCC could then have advised the facilities team, who in this instance would have visited the location and treated the contamination on the railhead with traffic film remover.

Above: Temporarily reduced to two cars, 11 is found at Nunnery on 16 March 1997. **Paul Jackson**

Right: The crumbled cab front of 118 is framed between 120 and another unidentified tram at Shalesmoor on 22 October 2015. **Paul Jackson**

Above: 118-1 is seen undergoing repairs at Nunnery depot on 10 December 2015. **Robert Pritchard**

JUST THE TICKET

In the first two years of operation, Supertram used ticket vending machines and validators supplied by Abberfield Technology of Australia. Each platform was provided with a bank of two ticket machines with a validator sandwiched between them. These machines sold adult £1 full fare (plus £1.50 tickets for some longer distance journeys where applicable) and 50p short hop, 25p concessionary and 15p child tickets. All coins from 5p to £1 were accepted but no change was given. After purchasing a ticket, the passenger had to insert it into the validator before boarding the tram. The journey then had to be completed within 90 minutes of validation. Tickets could also be bought from outlets including the South Yorkshire PTE Travel Information offices and retail outlets such as newsagents and convenience stores, with packs of ten single journey tickets available at a discount: ten £1 tickets for £7.50 and ten £1.50 tickets for £11.50.

Reliability of the original ticketing equipment was poor, and the machines were often slow to issue a ticket. Validators have never been in widespread use in the UK, and whereas in mainland Europe the passenger usually has simply to insert one end of the ticket into the validator whilst holding onto the other end, the Supertram validators required the whole ticket to be inserted and would then eject the ticket after stamping it with the date, time and code for the stop in question.

Unsurprisingly, within two years of the opening of Supertram the original ticket machines and validators were phased out during 1996–97, but rather than replace them with more sophisticated and expensive machines it was decided to abandon the use of ticket machines altogether in favour of on-board conductors who would issue and check tickets. This is largely in line with traditional UK tramway practice, except that the Supertram conductor's role is mainly in ticketing and customer care with the driver being responsible for opening and closing the doors and ensuring that it is safe to depart from each stop. This means that the conductor can continue with a ticketing transaction when the tram is standing at a stop if necessary, unlike on traditional trams where the conductor usually has to open and close the doors and tell the driver when it is safe to depart.

At Cathedral tram stop three sets of supports for the old ticket machines can still be seen – adapted into seats.

TICKETING AND FARES TODAY

At the time of this book going to press, in early 2020, an adult single for shorter journeys costs £1.90 (with a short journey return being offered for £3.20) and a longer journey single costs £2.60. Children and young people aged 5–18 pay a flat fare of 80p, although 11–18 year-olds must hold a South Yorkshire Megatravel or 16–18 Travel Pass (meaning that 11–18 year olds from outside South Yorkshire must pay the full adult fare). There is no longer journey return ticket as such, but various types of all-day ticket are available with varying levels of validity on other modes:

- Tram Only Dayrider: Valid only on Supertram, including the full tram-train route between Sheffield and Rotherham for a promotional period (£4.40);
- Silver Day: Valid on Supertram (including the tram-train route) and also on Stagecoach buses across South Yorkshire and in neighbouring areas (including Pontefract, Wakefield, Bawtry, Oldcotes, Blyth, Ranskill and in Derbyshire as far as Mastin Moor, Hillstown, Holmewood, Lower Pilsley, Tibshelf, Mickley, Clay Cross, Kelstedge and Holymoorside). Only valid on service X10 between Barnsley and Haigh (£4.90);
- CityWide Day: Valid on Supertram (including tram-train route as far as Meadowhall South/Tinsley) and all buses within the Sheffield city boundaries (£5.10);

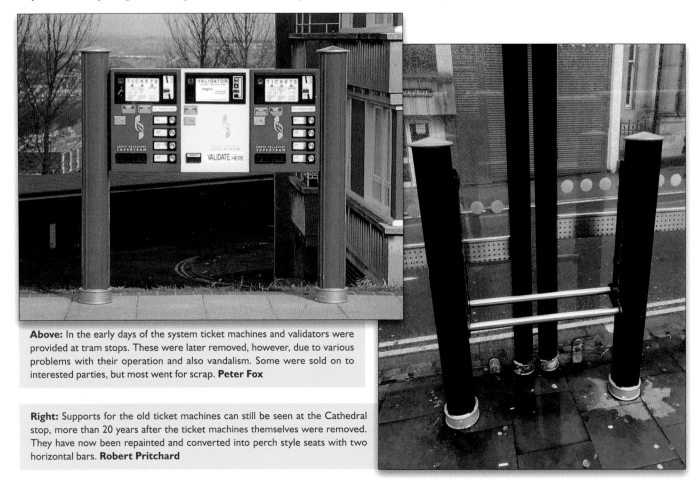

Above: In the early days of the system ticket machines and validators were provided at tram stops. These were later removed, however, due to various problems with their operation and also vandalism. Some were sold on to interested parties, but most went for scrap. **Peter Fox**

Right: Supports for the old ticket machines can still be seen at the Cathedral stop, more than 20 years after the ticket machines themselves were removed. They have now been repainted and converted into perch style seats with two horizontal bars. **Robert Pritchard**

- SYConnect Day: Valid on Supertram (including the full tram-train route) and all buses within South Yorkshire (£7);
- Gold Day: Valid on Supertram (including the full tram-train route) and all Stagecoach buses within South and West Yorkshire, Derbyshire, Nottinghamshire and as far as Gainsborough, Lincolnshire. Not valid on service X62, Pronto or in the Glossop area (£7.20); and
- SYConnect+ Day: As SYConnect Day but also valid on trains within South Yorkshire (£8.80).

In addition to those listed above a promotional After 8 ticket was introduced in December 2019. This is valid only for travel on Supertram (including the full tram-train route) and may only be purchased when boarding at either Parkgate or Rotherham Central. Valid only between 20.00 and the end of service (£2).

All of these tickets can be bought from tram conductors or (except for the Tram Only Dayrider and After 8 tickets) from drivers on participating bus operators. Until recently tram

Above: Although ticket vending machines are provided at tram stops in Edinburgh, Nottingham and Manchester, in Sheffield it was decided to do away with the slow and unreliable machines and replace them with on-board conductors, and nowadays ticket vending machines are only provided at Park & Ride sites. One such example, produced by Alfia, is seen at Halfway on 18 September 2019. **Ian Beardsley**

conductors could only accept cash, but new ticket issuing machines capable of accepting card payments were introduced (on a trial basis) during September 2019. To help make them easily identifiable to passengers, conductors involved in the trial wore pink hi-vis vests. Credit and debit cards are already accepted on First and Stagecoach buses in South Yorkshire.

Pensioners and disabled people who hold English National Concessionary Travel Scheme (ENCTS) passes from any other part of England may use their passes on Supertram between 09.30 and 23.00 on Mondays–Fridays and all day at weekends and bank holidays (unlike most other UK tram and light rail networks where only concessionary passes issued by the relevant local authority may be used). Concessionary pass holders from Scotland, Wales and Northern Ireland may not use their passes on Supertram (or anywhere else in England), however.

Full details of the range of one-day and longer period tickets available can be found at *www.travelsouthyorkshire.com/ticketspasses* and on the Supertram website at *www.stagecoachbus.com/supertram/ticket-info*.

PARK & RIDE SITES

South Yorkshire PTE operates seven Park & Ride sites located adjacent to tram stops, enabling motorists to park their cars and then continue their journey by tram. Users can purchase a ticket from the machines at the car parks for £4.50 that includes a day's parking and unlimited tram travel on the day of purchase. Car park only tickets are also available for £2.50. Other options include a pack of five Park & Ride tickets for £20, monthly tickets for £60.50 and quarterly tickets for £150.80.

The Park & Ride sites are located at Halfway, IKEA (adjacent to Carbrook/IKEA tram stop), Malin Bridge, Meadowhall, Middlewood, Nunnery Square and Valley Centertainment.

SUPERTRAM LINK BUSES

Stagecoach operates Supertram Link bus route SL1/SL1a between Middlewood and Stocksbridge, enabling residents of Stocksbridge and Deepcar to change onto the tram at Middlewood and reach destinations served by Supertram such as Meadowhall and the University of Sheffield. Routes SL1 and SL1a provide a combined service of five buses per hour on Mondays–Saturdays, three per hour on Sundays and one in the evening. Sheffield Tram & Bus Dayrider and all other ticket types that are valid on buses and trams can be used for through journeys involving Supertram and Supertram Link but unfortunately there are currently no single fares for such journeys. SL1/SL1a is the only Supertram Link route in existence at present, although two others have operated in the past: SL2 Malin Bridge–Stannington and SL3 Moss Way–Crystal Peaks–Killamarsh.

THE TRAMS KEEP RUNNING
WHATEVER THE
WEATHER.....

Whilst heavy falls of snow in South Yorkshire are not perhaps as common as they once were, there have still been a number of occasions when there has been heavy snow since the Supertram network opened. Generally, when this has been the case, trams have kept running (albeit with some delays, often when they get stuck behind stranded cars or buses, especially on the steep sections of Park Grange Road, City Road and Netherthorpe Road), whilst other public transport in the city has struggled, or even been suspended. The fact that Sheffield lies on seven hills often means that buses struggle during heavy snowfall. The worst snow in recent years was at the start of December 2010 when several inches fell in Sheffield – and much of it hung around for the next couple of weeks. As reported in **Today's Railways UK** magazine at the time "The trams themselves could cope with any amount of snow but the way certain motorists behave is very unhelpful in these conditions". Here we present a portfolio of shots from "snow events" in Sheffield.

Above: Snow hit Sheffield shortly before Supertram opened. On 25 February 1994 an unidentified tram crosses the bowstring bridge as it heads into the city centre on a test run. **Paul Jackson**

The tramway runs through open fields between White Lane and Birley Lane and also dips briefly into Derbyshire. This is by far the longest distance between stops on the network. On 7 February 2009 118 heads away from the camera towards Halfway. **Robert Pritchard**

Above: 112 leaves White Lane for Halfway on 5 January 2010. **Paul Jackson**

Above: 24 stands in a traffic jam near Hollinsend on 24 November 1996. **Paul Jackson**

Left: 108 is seen near White Lane during heavy snowfall on 6 January 2010. **Paul Jackson**

In a very rural scene, near Birley Lane, 108 heads for Halfway, passing 111 going to Malin Bridge on 7 February 2009. **Robert Pritchard**

Above: Meadowhall on 26 January 1995 sees 16 awaiting departure as a Class 142 leaves heading north. **Paul Jackson**

Right: 116 is seen in falling snow at Halfway on 1 March 2018. The state of the roads on this date meant that driving into the city was not an option! **Ian Beardsley**

123 leaves Gleadless Townend for Cathedral on 29 January 2015. **Paul Jackson**

118 is seen near Arbourthorne Road on its way to Halfway on 7 February 2009. **Robert Pritchard**

TRAM-TRAINS:
WHAT ARE THEY?

After a long wait, in October 2018 tram-trains started operating in South Yorkshire. But how did this whole project come about, and just what is a tram-train?

A tram-train is a light rail vehicle (LRV) built to main line railway standards and equipped to run both on tram tracks and on heavy rail lines that are shared with conventional trains. It is a development of the German Stadtbahn (city railway) concept of light rail networks running on a mixture of street track and dedicated rights of way, built to metro or rapid transit standards and in the latter case often running partly below ground.

The original concept of interurban tram vehicles running through to city centre metro or railway networks was pioneered in North America early in the 20th century (such as the Pacific Electric network in southern California, nicknamed the "Red Cars"), although the majority of systems were shut down by the 1960s. Manchester Metrolink (which has a mixture of street running and off-street tracks but no tunnel sections with stations apart from Piccadilly station undercroft) is an example of a network of this type. The Tyne & Wear Metro uses Stadtbahn type vehicles and has some Stadtbahn characteristics, with underground sections in Newcastle city centre, but no street running.

However, a conventional Stadtbahn type system consists entirely of tracks built for use exclusively by LRVs (although the Tyne & Wear Metro does run on Network Rail metals between Newcastle and Sunderland), whereas a tram-train can run through from the light rail onto the heavy rail network.

THE KARLSRUHE MODEL

Although Stadtbahn or interurban type networks have been around for several decades, the tram-train concept was pioneered in Karlsruhe, south-west Germany, in the early 1990s with the opening of the first route, Line B (now S4) between Karlsruhe and Gölshausen, in 1992. Since then the Karlsruhe Stadtbahn system has continually expanded and is now a comprehensive network of routes connecting Karlsruhe with nearby towns and villages such as Rastatt, Baden-Baden and Heilbronn using a mixture of on-street tram tracks and heavy rail lines (the latter mostly shared with conventional trains including heavy freight and high speed services but with some lines used exclusively by the tram-trains). This type of network is referred to as the "Karlsruhe Model" or Karlsruher Modell in German. Another notable feature of the Karlsruhe network is that it uses two different electrification systems: 750 V DC on the light rail sections (both on-street and on dedicated rights of way) and 15 kV 16.7 Hz (the standard voltage on the German national rail network) on the heavy rail sections. Because of this, the Karlsruhe tram-train fleet is equipped to run on both voltages. Today, the Karlsruhe network uses

Left: Vossloh Citylink NET 2012 car 371 waits at Karlsruhe Hbf with an S1 service to Hochstetten on 11 July 2019. On the right is Bombardier ET 2010 car 940. **Alan Yearsley**

GT8-100D/2S-M car 866 arrives at Mühlacker with an S9 service to Bruchsal on 8 December 2017. This route operates entirely on heavy rail tracks but some other routes include a mixture of heavy and light rail metals. Note the freight train on the left. **Keith Fender**

a variety of vehicles built by Bombardier, Duewag/Siemens, and Vossloh-Kiepe.

More recently, at least three other German cities – Chemnitz, Kassel and Saarbrücken – have also developed tram-train networks, albeit on a smaller scale. These networks each use a different type of bi-mode electro-diesel or dual voltage LRV. The more established Kassel RegioTram system uses 28 RegioCitadis LRVs supplied by Alstom; ten of these are electro-diesel bi-modes with roof-mounted diesel power packs and have been used to extend services onto non-electrified parts of the regional rail network such as Line RT4 Kassel–Wolfhagen. Dual voltage RegioCitadis cars are also used on the RandstadRail tram-train routes between Den Haag (The Hague) and Zoetermeer in the Netherlands.

The Chemnitz system, known in German as the Chemnitzer Modell, uses only bi-mode electro-diesel LRVs, in this case Stadler-built Citylink units as used for the new Sheffield–Rotherham tram-train scheme, although unlike the British version the Chemnitz ones are fitted with roof-mounted diesel power packs to operate on the regional rail network. The Chemnitz system has allowed passengers from surrounding regional towns to have a "one seat ride" to the city centre; the main station being sited around 1 km from the centre. Passenger numbers have grown substantially on the routes on which the bi-mode Citylinks are now used. Chemnitz has an ambitious five-stage plan to build a regional network, reopening some lines that closed more than 20 years ago and adding new sections of city tramway at the same time.

Saarbrücken, whilst only using 750 V DC on the on-street sections, mainly in the city centre, is unusual amongst European tram-train operations in that it operates across the border into the French town of Sarreguemines. German main line 15 kV AC electrification is used for this section. The Saarbahn network has been slowly expanded since it first opened in the late 1990s and is operated with a Bombardier-built fleet of Flexity Link dual voltage LRVs.

BI-MODE AND DIESEL TRAM-TRAINS

Elsewhere in Germany, Siemens Combino Duo bi-mode 600 V DC electro-diesel tram-trains are used on the metre gauge tramways in the former East German town of Nordhausen. These operate in electric mode on the tram network and in diesel mode on the Harzer Schmalspurbahn (Harz narrow gauge) network between Nordhausen Nord station and Ilfeld Neanderklinik.

Above: Aarhus in Denmark uses Stadler tram-trains on its new system. On 5 February 2018 Variobahn tram 1209/1109 arrives at Dokk1 with a service to Aarhus main station. **Robert Pritchard**

Zwickau, also in the former East Germany, has implemented a reverse of the Karlsruhe model, known as the Zwickau Model or Zwickauer Modell, whereby conventional heavy rail diesel railcars operated by Die Länderbahn (branded as Vogtlandbahn) have been adapted to run through onto the tramway network (which are sometimes referred to as train-trams, since they are effectively a tram-train in reverse). Whereas all other tram-train networks in Germany, apart from Nordhausen, are standard (1435 mm) gauge, Zwickau has mixed gauge track on the sections used by both types of vehicle with the conventional trams being metre (1000 mm) gauge and the Vogtlandbahn DMUs using the 1435 mm gauge rails. Die Länderbahn operates two routes starting in Zwickau town centre: RB1 to Falkenstein and Kraslice (Czech Republic) and RB2 to Plauen, Adorf and Cheb (Czech Republic). Stadler built Regio-Shuttle DMUs started operating these services from December 2019.

There are several more tram-train systems in Europe and many more planned; in France dual voltage LRVs are used from Nantes, albeit on routes that entirely comprise former main line railway. In Spain, Alicante has a tram-train system using bi-mode electro-diesel LRVs although conversion of the metre gauge former railway routes from Benidorm to Denia has yet to be completed. In Denmark, the second largest city Aarhus is developing an extensive "Letbane" (light rail) system with a mix of Variobahn and Tango trams to service outlying areas towards Odder and Grenaa, some over railway lines which have been adapted to accommodate tram-trains. A similar system is due to open in Denmark's third city, Odense, in 2020.

Outside Europe, examples of tram-train type systems in the USA include Capitol MetroRail in Austin, Texas and the River Line between Trenton and Camden, New Jersey, both of which use diesel units, and the electric TRAX light rail network in Salt Lake City, Utah. The Keihan Electric Railway in Japan is an interurban network with some tram-train characteristics.

Left: Chemnitz Stadler Citylink tram-train 438 approaches Chemnitz Hbf on the new connecting line between the tramway and the DB rail network with a C13 service to Burgstädt on 2 April 2019. Just visible on the left is ADtranz Variobahn tram 902. **Keith Fender**

TRAM-TRAIN
TECHNOLOGY

The key differences between a tram or LRV and a train are normally:

- Vehicle construction methods with the light rail vehicle being lighter and therefore requiring less power to accelerate but also reducing crashworthiness in collisions with other trains or road vehicles on crossings.
- Power source; most city tram systems use DC current at relatively low voltages. Whilst new build tramways normally use 750 or 850 V DC nominal voltage some older systems use lower voltages such as 600 V DC. On the other hand, heavy rail EMUs all use much higher voltages with 25 kV AC standard in the UK and many EU countries. Even those countries that use DC power for main line railways mostly use 3000 V DC (the Netherlands and parts of France are the exception with 1500 V DC still in use). Tram-trains need to combine operation on tramways and main line railways. This is usually done by having electrical systems that allow operation on both, normally necessitating provision of a heavier transformer than needed by a simple city tram LRV, or by providing a source of power for operation away from the city centre using diesel power packs. Battery power is increasingly likely to be used especially for relatively short sections (up to 20 km each way) – the planned Stadler Citylink LRVs being acquired by Transport for Wales will include battery powerpacks for use on non-electrified sections of the routes they operate.
- Flexibility – heavy rail vehicles are designed for use on a wide variety of track geometry, sometimes aligned for 250 km/h+ use, and with complex heavy rail points and switches. Trams tend to use simpler track layouts with tighter curves, and in city centres they often run on track that is set into the street. Tram-train LRVs need to be able to cope with both these situations and are normally equipped with specially designed wheelsets that enable safe operation on the main line and on city centre tram tracks.
- Signalling and control systems – for city operation most tramways rely on line of sight with some roadside signals for drivers. Tram-trains on the other hand have to be able to operate on the main line, operating track circuits and equipped with whatever the relevant safety systems are. The German tram-trains in Karlsruhe, Chemnitz and Kassel all are equipped with the German main line standard Indusi safety system.
By Keith Fender

Above: LRV construction at Stadler Valencia in January 2019; this tram-train is for the future Alicante–Denia route in Spain. **Keith Fender**

Above: Chemnitz Citylink roof-mounted diesel power pack. **Keith Fender**

Left: Wheel profile: Chemnitz Citylink showing the different profile – on the inside of the wheel it has to accommodate street running so is narrower at the rim than at the axle as the picture shows. **Keith Fender**

A TRAM-TRAIN PILOT FOR PENISTONE?

In 2008 the then Labour Transport Secretary Ruth Kelly announced plans to order five diesel-powered tram-trains for the Sheffield–Huddersfield via Penistone line at a cost of £25 million, funded by the Department for Transport and Network Rail. The two-year experiment was planned to start in late 2010, with the tram-trains being leased by train operator Northern. This would have seen tram-trains operating entirely on Network Rail metals, but was intended to gain experience in operating vehicles of this type in readiness for a possible later phase involving through running between the national rail network and the Supertram system.

Tram-trains have the advantage of being lighter than a conventional train, and this can help save on track maintenance costs. However, apart from this there would probably have been very little benefit in using tram-trains on the Penistone line, which only runs close to the Supertram system at Meadowhall (where the Barnsley line is at the opposite side of the station to the tram terminus) and at Sheffield Midland (where the tram tracks are at a much higher level than the station itself). Tram-trains are also usually designed to operate with lower platforms than conventional trains, so all or part of the platform at each station along the route would have had to be lowered (reducing the length of platform available for use by conventional trains at stations between Sheffield and Barnsley, which are also served by other trains). Tram-trains do not usually have toilets, which the DMUs currently used on the Penistone line do have (although some of the tram-train vehicles used on longer-distance routes in Karlsruhe have toilets). It is likely that many passengers on the route would not have been happy about the removal of this facility, particularly those travelling all the way between Sheffield and Huddersfield, a journey time of around 1h15.

The Penistone line project was heavily criticised by many commentators. Eventually, concerns about the cost and practicalities of tram-train operation over the Sheffield–Huddersfield line, including difficulties in procuring diesel tram-trains (the same type used in Kassel, Germany were favoured, but these were no longer available as their roof-mounted diesel engines were no longer compliant with new emissions regulations), led to this plan being abandoned by the autumn of 2009 in favour of the current scheme for a service between Sheffield and Rotherham Parkgate, which eventually received the go-ahead in May 2012.

Suitable for tram-trains? An unidentified 3-car Northern Class 144 "Pacer" DMU crosses Lockwood Viaduct with the 17.37 Sheffield–Huddersfield on 7 May 2018. Train operator Northern planned to withdraw all of its Pacer units on this line by the end of May 2020. **Robert France**

THE ROTHERHAM TRAM-TRAIN
PROJECT

The first extension to the Supertram network was the tram-train pilot to Rotherham, opened in October 2018, almost three years later than had been planned. The scheme was intended to provide the first transport service in the UK to combine a street tramway with the national rail network. The programme involved modifying the existing national rail infrastructure, modifying the tram network and depot, and purchasing a new fleet of vehicles capable of running on both networks. Services are now operating as part of a two-year trial, fully funded by the Department for Transport. South Yorkshire PTE (SYPTE) and Stagecoach are fully expecting to continue to operate the trial after this time (subject to it being commercially viable), at least until the end of the current Stagecoach Supertram concession in March 2024.

The objective of the project was to demonstrate the costs, benefits, safety requirements and required standard changes for operating a standard continental design of tram-train on the national rail network. The concept would provide additional capacity on the existing rail network, where there is often limited room for expansion.

BACKGROUND

Following the cancellation of the Penistone pilot, the Rotherham scheme was given the go-ahead in 2012, with Transport Minister Norman Baker giving the green light on 17 May. Services were due to commence in 2015, by which time the existing Northern Rail franchise was scheduled to have finished, hence

responsibility for leading the delivery of the new vehicles and sponsoring the project (in collaboration with Network Rail, Stagecoach Supertram and Northern Rail) was given to SYPTE. Northern would therefore have little involvement in the day-to-day running of tram-train: the tram-trains would

Above: Some of the key players involved in the tram-train project pose for photos at the Parkgate terminus on the first morning of operation on 25 October 2018, from left to right the then Minister of Transport Jo Johnson (brother of Boris, who became Prime Minister the following year), Stagecoach Supertram Managing Director Tim Bilby, South Yorkshire PTE Executive Director Stephen Edwards, Mayor of the Sheffield City Region (and Labour MP for Barnsley) Dan Jarvis and Network Rail Route Managing Director LNE&EM Region Rob McIntosh. **Robert Pritchard**

As dawn breaks on the opening day of the tram-train service, 25 October 2018, 399 204 awaits departure from Nunnery depot with a special service to Parkgate for invited guests. **Robert Pritchard**

Left: Minister of Transport Jo Johnson and Mayor of Sheffield City Region Dan Jarvis pose alongside 399 204 at Parkgate on the opening day. **Robert Pritchard**

fit around the existing Northern timetable rather than vice-versa, so the rail operator's main involvement was with changes needed at Rotherham Central station (which Northern managed). The objective of the pilot scheme was to determine the practical and operational issues of extending tram-trains from the national railway network to on-street running, and of running trams and heavy rail vehicles over the same heavy rail infrastructure.

There were a number of practicalities that would be investigated by the pilot, practicalities that could not necessarily be directly transferred to British operational circumstances from Continental experience in places such as Karlsruhe. Regardless of the higher end-loading resistance required for heavy rail operation, the Supertram fleet was not fitted with the GSM-R radio system and modern signalling safety devices used on Network Rail routes with their higher speeds. Their doors are flush with the platform edges on the Supertram system and at a level to match those platforms: therefore it would be necessary to install a modified platform at the existing station at Rotherham Central, plus at the new tram-only terminus at Parkgate. The trial would also gauge passenger perception, including reaction to the type of vehicles used and the improvements delivered by better penetration of city centres.

Another practicality to be investigated was the need to find a wheel profile that would run satisfactorily both on Network Rail track and on the Supertram network. This was one of the reasons for the trial to take place in South Yorkshire – another possibility would have been for the trial to be in Greater Manchester, but here Metrolink already uses a similar wheel profile to the neighbouring heavy rail network.

Above: Expectant passengers wait for 399 203 to arrive at Cathedral, prior to it forming the 11.39 to Parkgate on 25 October 2018, the first day of tram-train operation. **Robert Pritchard**

Left: Progress with construction of the new low-level tram-train platforms at Rotherham Central, just south of the main line platforms, is seen on 20 April 2018. At this stage the frames of small waiting shelters had been added, but the platforms were yet to be surfaced. **Mike Haddon**

Left & below: Stagecoach's tram-train timetable and guide, for the launch in October 2018 and the revised timetable from December 2019. **Courtesy Stagecoach Supertram**

Your TRAM TRAIN
LAUNCHES 25TH OCTOBER
supertram.com

Connecting **Rotherham** with the centre of **Sheffield**

TRAM TRAIN
In partnership with
NetworkRail

Tram Train
timetable & fare guide

Stagecoach
SUPERTRAM
TRAM TRAIN

AMENDED TIMETABLE
WITH LATER SERVICES!

- Sheffield Cathedral
- Fitzalan Square
- Nunnery Square
- Arena / Olympic Legacy Park
- Valley Centertainment
- Meadowhall South / Tinsley
- Rotherham Central
- **Rotherham Parkgate**
  (refer to network map for full route)

27 MINS JOURNEY TIME

up to **3 PER HOUR**

From **Sunday 15th December 2019**

The cost of the pilot in May 2012 was quoted as £58 million. The project included 750 V DC overhead electrification of the Network Rail line from a connection with the Supertram Meadowhall route at Tinsley, through Rotherham Central to Parkgate retail park, and the provision of seven tram-trains: four to cover the tram-train pilot and three to provide an augmented service on existing Supertram routes. The £58 million was broken down as:

- £18M for electrification work and other modifications to railway infrastructure;
- £30M for the seven tram-trains; and
- £10M for other Supertram work such as modifications to the depot, driver recruitment and training and drawing up standards specifically for this operation.

The scheduled inauguration of the tram-train service in 2015 was planned to provide a tram every 20 minutes between Parkgate and Sheffield Cathedral, and a total journey time of around 25 minutes. The service would be required to mix satisfactorily with the three DMU trains an hour in each direction that already stop at Rotherham Central, plus a number of freight services that also use the line.

A procurement competition identified Vossloh as the lead bidder for the seven tram-train cars, which were expected to be operated by Stagecoach Supertram (with tickets fully integrated with Supertram). The trial was originally proposed to commence in December 2015 and was to be fully funded by the Government. It would run for two years, with a view to permanent operation if successful.

The 750 V DC electrification would match the Supertram operation and was, in theory at least, the cheaper option: 25 kV AC feeder stations are very expensive and one would have been needed for what would have been a relatively short section of electrified track. However, the equipment would be designed for straightforward conversion to 25 kV in the future and the vehicles would be dual voltage so they would be compatible in future with any 25 kV electrification of the Midland Main Line that could then extend onwards to Doncaster/Leeds (however, the MML electrification to Nottingham and Sheffield was cancelled by the Government in 2017 so this is unlikely in the medium-term).

Above: Taken from the footpath on the Tinsley Viaduct, 399 203 leaves the conventional tramway (Meadowhall route) and runs onto the newly-created Tinsley chord as it heads to Parkgate with a test run on 19 July 2018. The Meadowhall South/Tinsley stop can be seen in the background. **Mike Haddon**

Right: Shortly after test running started to Parkgate, 399 203 awaits departure back to Cathedral on 26 July 2018, as 144 017 passes with the 11.51 Hull–Sheffield. Aldwarke Steelworks dominates the background. **Ian Beardsley**

Left: 399 203 turns sharply onto the Tinsley chord on its way to Parkgate on 24 March 2019. **Robert Pritchard**

Below: A wider view of the Tinsley chord, with the former GCR line to the right foreground. 399 203 heads for Parkgate, again on 25 October 2018. **Robert Pritchard**

Manchester University was employed to investigate the critical wheel-rail profile. Operating over two systems with differing rail profiles is tricky, and needs careful assessment. Fitting a wheel profile suitable for both tramway and main line track is essential, and one of the major issues to be addressed by the pilot.

Just over a year after the go-ahead, on 19 June 2013, Transport Minister Norman Baker visited Sheffield to sign off the order for the seven tram-train vehicles from Vossloh.

COSTS RISE OUT OF CONTROL AS DELAYS MOUNT

The Rotherham tram-train scheme has not been without controversy, particularly with regard to several delays and rising costs. By its very nature it was always going to be a very bespoke scheme, and there seemed to be much underestimation in the original figures, and mistakes made throughout the process that further mired the project with delays. This would be Network Rail's first electrification scheme at 750 V DC overhead (contrasting sharply with NR's usual 25 kV AC), and many lessons would be learnt throughout the process. NR said that it was the change to a 750 V DC system that could be adapted to AC that caused the main increases in costs, and also a delay of around 18 months while additional safety validation work for this system was undertaken. A significant number of scope changes to the project also added considerable extra costs.

Delays in the design of the works needed to adapt the heavy rail network for tram-train operation led to the start date being put back several times. In March 2015 Network Rail submitted a Transport & Works Act Order application to the DfT for the 400 m Tinsley chord to connect the Sheffield–Meadowhall tram route to the former Great Central Woodburn Junction–Rotherham Central freight line, which was granted in November of that year. In 2011 the DfT had set a budget of £15 million for NR's infrastructure works, later increased to £18M. By November 2014 NR had increased its estimate for

the cost of the project to £44.9 million, and by December 2016 this had risen again to £75.1 million. Funding was shared between the DfT and NR (having originally been planned to be met entirely by the DfT) with the DfT providing £45.3 million and NR £29.8 million.

The National Audit Office (NAO) published an independent report into spiralling costs in July 2017. Costs had risen to over five times the original budget. The independent report criticised the Government and Network Rail for losing control of the scheme, which was originally scheduled for completion in December 2015 and then December 2016, with the benefit-cost ratio having dropped to just 0.31. The original benefit-cost ratio was 1.0. Under pressure of rising costs, then Rail Minister Paul Maynard was given the option of cancelling the scheme in 2014, but it was felt that such a move would cause reputational damage so it was decided to push on. In July 2016, the Permanent Secretary endorsed the DfT's recommendation that the project be scrapped, but the Rail Minister did not agree and requested that Network Rail meet the funding shortfall.

The key findings of the NAO's investigation were as follows:

- The pilot project aimed to test the viability of operating tram-trains in the UK. The Government's approval was based on the wider strategic benefits of rolling-out schemes to other cities to reinvigorate under-used rail lines, better penetrate city centre markets and release capacity at main line railway stations. The Government and Network Rail agreed that a pilot project was the best way to test whether the tramway technology could be extended onto national rail lines, and to develop new industry standards.
- The DfT accepted the project's wider financial benefits were uncertain. The business case for the proposed scheme was based on the benefits to local transport users, such as reduced journey times. The benefit-cost ratio (BCR) of 1.0 fell into the "low" value-for-money category, but the Government considered the wider

benefits of the pilot, such as lower industry costs and economic benefits, to be "very uncertain". In May 2012, HM Treasury approved the project "on an exceptional basis" to allow a more detailed evaluation of the value for money of tram-train schemes.

- The Department and Network Rail initially agreed a budget of £15 million to modify the national rail infrastructure. In May 2012, NR estimated the project would cost £18.7 million but expected to make efficiency savings. By November 2014, NR established that costs had exceptionally increased to some £44.9 million, an increase of 199% against budget. In July 2012, the DfT announced that it expected that the national rail line would be electrified after 2019 and asked Network Rail to undertake additional works to adapt the tram-train service.

- On 28 November 2014 the then Permanent Secretary concluded the project's rationale had not changed and recognised that cancelling the project would cause reputational damage. The DfT agreed to provide cash funding, capped at £45.3 million because NR, now it had been reclassified as a public body, could no longer increase its borrowing to finance cost increases in the tram-train project.

- In 2015, the DfT introduced new arrangements to strengthen its governance of the project following a review that identified concerns with the way the project was set-up and governed.

- In June 2016, NR reported that forecast costs had risen further, by up to £25 million. NR established that works were more complex than it anticipated at the design stage, that it had incurred additional costs in dealing with the condition of assets and the technical "innovations" required more time than originally expected. At the start of the project, NR did not have a full understanding of the costs, and revised its forecasts as it identified the technical challenges involved in testing the technology.

- In July 2016, the then Permanent Secretary recommended stopping further work on the project. The DfT's Rail Investment Board, with the endorsement of the Permanent Secretary, recommended stopping the project as many of the lessons of using tram-trains in the UK had already been learnt. The Board stated that this would release at least £20 million from the Department's budget but the majority of the £25 million already spent by NR would be lost. The DfT did not prepare or request a revised business case at this point.

- In September 2016 the Transport Minister did not accept the Accounting Officer's recommendation and asked NR to meet the funding shortfall. This decision was based on the need for the lessons learned from the completed pilot to be available for the development of further schemes. In October 2016, the DfT recalculated the BCR to provide assurance that the decision could be defended on value for money grounds. It calculated that the BCR of the remaining works was 1.49, treating committed expenditure as a sunk cost. The BCR of the overall programme had fallen to 0.31, in terms of the local public transport case.

- NR agreed to fund the remainder of the project. It allocated £4.6 million from its renewals budget to address issues with the poor condition of existing assets. It proposed to complete the remaining construction works by reprioritising funding from its wider enhancement programme and reallocating approximately £21.9 million to the tram-train project. The Minister endorsed this approach in March 2017.

- The DfT and NR then expected the works to cost £75.1 million, an increase of 401% on the original budget. NR revised its plans in December 2016 and increased its estimate of project costs. The works were expected to be completed in May 2018, allowing the service to start in summer 2018.

Above: 399 203 is about to pass under College Road bridge at Rotherham Central station with a service for Cathedral on 27 June 2019. Note how the equipment cabinets and repeater signals have been raised on stilts following flooding over recent years here. **Robert Pritchard**

Left: A number of passengers wait to board 399 206 at Rotherham Central as it heads to Cathedral on 27 June 2019. The barriers between the tracks to dissuade people from crossing the tracks from the low level platforms can clearly be seen. **Robert Pritchard**

- The DfT and NR have learned lessons from the pilot but it is too early to determine whether the project will realise the wider strategic benefits. The DfT and NR have begun to capture the operational issues involved in using tram-trains in the UK and have, for example, established new technical standards for the signalling. NR has shared lessons learned with other tram-train promoters. The DfT has not yet evaluated the value for money of the pilot project or the extent to which it will reduce the costs of introducing similar schemes in other cities.

Reacting to the report, Stephen Edwards, Executive Director of South Yorkshire PTE, said: "Network Rail seriously underestimated the resources required and has clearly struggled to overcome these complexities".

NEW INFRASTRUCTURE AND POWER

Network Rail delivered the infrastructure modifications required for the project, the highlights being as follows:

- Electrification of the route at 750 V DC and new signalling power supply points. The 750 V DC would match the rest of the tram network, but with provision made for conversion to the railway standard 25 kV AC in the future, should the railway line through Rotherham ever be electrified (now seen as unlikely in the medium-term). A number of considerations had to be taken into account during the electrification work, for example the fact that a tram's pantograph is bigger than those normally seen on heavy rail Electric Multiple Units, which affected gauge clearance. There is also more sway and lateral movement with a tram.

- Construction of a new DC substation to power the route at Ickles, close to where the "Old Road" crosses the line (near Holmes Junction). Much of the equipment is raised on platforms as part of flood mitigation measures. The Ickles substation interfaces with Supertram's own substations at Blackburn Meadows and Carbrook.

- The main new infrastructure is the 160 m double-track chord at Tinsley, almost directly beneath the M1 motorway viaduct, that connects the tramway with the railway network. This features an 80 m radius curve following a very tight 25 m radius turnout that wouldn't be suitable for use by trains but is fine for trams, which are designed to run on much more severe track geometry. Perhaps highlighting some of the challenges facing those involved with the project, the chord has an amazing 12 different

Shortly after departure from Rotherham Central tram-trains pass Rotherham United's £17 million New York stadium, which opened in 2012 and has a capacity of 12 000. On 27 June 2019 399 206 runs past the stadium on the short section with three tracks (the line to the left then becomes the single-track Holmes chord line) with a late afternoon service for Cathedral. **Robert Pritchard**

Making its first, and for some time its last, public trip to Parkgate, 399 204 heads away from the camera towards Rotherham Central underneath Bessemer Way on 25 October 2018. Templeborough Biomass Power Plant can be seen to the right and in the distance the "Old Road" freight-only railway line crosses the tram-train route. The route is double track here with both lines electrified but the overhead gantries are single cantilevers on the north side. **Chris Booth**

operational and maintenance boundaries that have arisen from engineering and operational regimes in the tightly constrained site, requiring proactive management and a 250 m overlap of tramway and railway.

- Changes to a number of structures were needed. College Road bridge at Rotherham Central was raised (but will need to be raised again should the overhead ever be converted to 25 kV AC), and the track was lowered underneath the Greasbrough Road bridge and the Ickles Viaduct (where the "Old Road" crosses). The tracks through Rotherham Central could not be lowered because of a history of flooding at this location, and indeed flooding hit Rotherham Central during autumn 2019 to such an extent that the tram-train platforms were submerged! The pedestrian bridge at Parkgate required a new deck.

- New low-height platforms at Rotherham Central station, along with shelters and access ramps down from the national rail platforms. The new platforms have been given the numbers 3 and 4 and have their own waiting shelters and digital train information boards. They are accessible via the main entrance and then the rail platforms, having a height of 390 mm compared to 915 mm for the rail platforms. Barriers have been installed between the tracks beside the light rail platforms to discourage people from stepping off the low-height platforms into the path of trains. NR described these as one of the most fundamental design challenges to be overcome by the project, but now they are complete the barriers stand out as a unique feature and a case study of what can be done. Other options considered but discounted included platform screen doors, as seen on parts of the London Underground; however, these could have introduced more risk.

- The new single platform station on a short spur at Rotherham Parkgate, for use by tram-trains only.

- Raised check rails were fitted alongside switches and crossings because of the recessed flange profile (for street running) of the tram-trains and the perceived risk of splitting points. Instead of being level with the running railhead, the check rails have to be raised by a minimum of 40 mm. This means that certain types of train are now prohibited from using the route, including snowploughs (when in ploughing mode), Class 33 diesel locos with unmodified lifeguards and Class 91 electric locos (the latter two classes not being likely to need to use the route). In service it has been found that tram-trains are experiencing increased flange wear over switches and crossings at around 40 mph, rather than the 10–15 mph of tramway operation.

Modifications to signalling included a change from track circuits to axle counters to give immunity from OLE interference, while Vehicle Identification System (VIS) loop magnets are used for tram detection and to prevent misrouting.

Network Rail worked with colleagues in the North-East to identify what could be done to mitigate stray current (not an issue with AC overhead electrification) following experience with the Tyne & Wear Metro Sunderland extension, which uses 1500 V DC. Steel sleepers on the route were also a consideration in this regard, and the use of axle counters negates any interaction between the DC power and track circuits.

The original concept envisaged new electrification would be controlled from the Supertram control room at Nunnery depot. This was later changed to Network Rail control due to Electricity at Work Regulations compliance, competence and experience issues. York assumed traction control of the NR infrastructure and Supertram remains in control up to the interface boundary.

TESTING AHEAD OF THE SERVICE STARTING

After years of delays, the tram-train service finally commenced on 25 October 2018, with a celebratory atmosphere on board trams during the day, a ministerial visit, glorious weather, and, unfortunately, a serious accident.

The opening followed several months of testing and crew training. The tram-train route between Parkgate and Tinsley was handed over for testing to take place on 8 May 2018. In the early hours of 10 May the first tram-train (399 202, the first to receive the tram-train wheel profile) ventured onto Network Rail metals as far as the Magna science park at Templeborough. The recovery of a failed tram was also simulated during testing on the night of 11 May using 66156. In case of failure, the favoured option for vehicle recovery is to use another tram-train, but if power is not available rescue with a locomotive is

Above: The immediate aftermath of the accident at Staniforth Road on the afternoon of 25 October 2018. 399 204 collided with the flatbed lorry, seen bottom right, and as a result was lifted off the tracks and derailed. **Ian Beardsley**

Left: The damage to the front end of 399 204 is evident as it ended up embedded in the lorry. **Ian Beardsley**

Below: The rare sight of one of the original Siemens trams coupled to one of the tram-trains. 121, which had been following 399 204 with a Yellow Route service, was coupled up to drag the tram-train back onto the tracks at dusk. **Ian Beardsley**

possible. Stagecoach developed an emergency coupler that fits over the screwlink drawbar and enables a loco, such as the ubiquitous freight Class 66, to drag a tram away – or alternatively to propel it back onto the Tinsley chord.

399 204 became the second vehicle to receive the tram-train wheel profiles. Testing with the vehicles to Rotherham started in June, 399 202 becoming the first to visit Parkgate on 5 June. Daylight testing commenced from 16 July and then crew training started shortly afterwards. Shadow running to the full timetable started in late September, around four weeks ahead of the launch, with crew training continuing during this time. The Stadler tram-trains had, however, already started in operation on the established Supertram network in September 2017.

OPENING DAY LAUNCH MARRED BY ACCIDENT

The historic opening day, Thursday 25 October 2018, dawned clear and sunny. This date was chosen because of the availability of the Minister for Transport, Jo Johnson, who was at Parkgate to greet an early morning special for the media, stakeholders and invited guests. This left Nunnery tram depot at 08.00 formed of set 399 204 (Supertram fleet No. 204). Speaking at Parkgate the Minister was bullish, saying that he hoped the pilot would be followed by other similar schemes in other parts of the country. Sheffield City Region Mayor, Dan Jarvis, said the trial placed South Yorkshire at the forefront of transport innovation in the country.

The Minister and other guests then travelled on this set back to Cathedral, before 399 204 ran empty out of service back to the depot. The first public service left Cathedral at 09.39, formed of 399 203. A queuing system was in place for this service at Cathedral, but all those who wished to travel on the first service could do so. This was followed by departures at 10.01 (set 399 202) and 10.27 (set 399 201), before 399 203 returned for the 10.39 departure and the pattern of operation for the opening day was thus set.

In the early afternoon 399 201 was swapped for 399 204, but disaster was to strike 399 204 on its return journey, the 14.59 from Parkgate – this tram's very first public service from Parkgate. At around 15.20, and with about 80 passengers on board (several of whom were standing), 399 204 collided with a flatbed lorry that had jumped traffic lights on Staniforth Road, between Attercliffe and Woodbourn Road stops on the Meadowhall tram line. The tram-train was travelling at around 20 mph and derailed, coming to a rest some distance from the track, embedded into the lorry. Fortunately, no-one was seriously injured, although one person had to be taken to hospital and some others were treated for minor injuries at the scene. Both the Parkgate tram-train service and Yellow Route Meadowhall trams beyond Cricket Inn Road were suspended for the rest of 25 October, resuming during late morning the following day, once damaged track had been replaced.

The accident was one of the worst that Supertram had ever seen. The impact was significant, and unusual, as the square-sided flatbed lorry managed to catch the tram-train just above the anti-climb bars and embedded itself into the vehicle body profile. The body warped, but the actual superstructure remained intact. Stagecoach later said that the tram-train stood up well to the accident, and had it been an older Siemens tram involved, not built to railway crashworthiness standards, then the driver would almost certainly have lost his legs. In a personal impact statement read to the court during the trial of the lorry driver, the driver of 399 204 said that he was thankful he was driving one of the new vehicles.

It was stated shortly after the accident that the tram driver had a "clear to proceed" signal at the road junction, and the lorry had gone through a red light – Network Rail stating that it suspected that the driver had fallen asleep. The lorry driver was later charged with driving without due care and attention, and driving through a red light. At the trial in August 2019 Mr Hague, 60, of Rotherham, was found guilty of driving through a red light and ordered to pay a fine of £250 plus costs, along with three points on his licence. The costs of repairs to the tram, estimated at £1 million, were covered by his insurance company.

There was unfortunately a second accident involving a tram-train (399 202) at the same crossing on 30 November 2018. Whilst working the 16.09 Parkgate–Cathedral at dusk, 399 202 collided with a car at the same crossing. The car was severely damaged and all three occupants were taken to hospital. The tram-train did not derail, but had to be jacked up to remove debris from underneath it, and suffered front end damage. This resulted in a hybrid tram being formed (see Stadler tram-trains section).

Left: On 29 November 2019 399 203 passes the point of the accident at the Staniforth Road crossing as it heads to Cathedral. The white building above the tram is the local Aaliyah Mosque and Islamic Centre. At the time just two tram-train services per hour were in operation due to modifications being carried out to the tram-trains. **Robert Pritchard**

Below: Following the collision with a car at the Staniforth Road crossing on 30 November 2018 399 202 "Theo" is jacked up to remove debris from underneath the vehicle. **Ian Beardsley**

Right: 399 204 returned to traffic on 19 January 2020 on the tram-train route. On 27 February 2020 it is seen at Cathedral with the 17.39 to Parkgate as 119 heads for Malin Bridge. The end illustrated is 999004, which was rebuilt by Stadler in Spain. **Robert Pritchard**

THE TRAM-TRAIN SERVICE

The tram-train service runs to a slightly different timetable compared to the main network, with no early morning service on Sundays or on Sunday evenings (in the first year). For the first year of operation the service operated three times an hour, seven days a week, but unfortunately not at evenly-spaced intervals as it has to fit in between the (unevenly-spaced) three-train-per-hour local Northern service trains on the Rotherham Central line. On Mondays–Saturdays departures from Cathedral are at xx.00, xx.27 and xx.39 and from Parkgate at xx.09, xx.31 and xx.59.

The first service leaves Cathedral at 05.27 and the last at 22.44. The first from Parkgate is at 05.59 and the last at 23.16. Initially, times were almost identical on Sundays, but the service only ran between around 08.30 and 18.00, the first service from Cathedral is 08.27, the last at 18.00 and from Parkgate the first is 08.59 and the last at 18.31. When there is engineering

Following the opening day accident, which put 399 204 out of action for more than a year, 399 206 was converted from a tram to a tram-train. On its first day following conversion, it waits at Cathedral with the 15.27 to Parkgate on 3 November 2018, as 107 leaves for Malin Bridge. **Robert Pritchard**

work on the main line through Meadowhall that sees trains being diverted via Rotherham Central and Woodburn Junction, the tram-train service is reduced to two trains per hour on Sundays.

To enable a three-tram service, turnaround times at both ends are tight (they couldn't be long at Cathedral in any case, as this is a busy stop with 12 trams per hour in each direction, including Purple Route trams also terminating and reversing). As tram-train adds extra capacity to the Meadowhall line there were some changes to the Supertram timetable as a result, the most significant being that Purple Route trams no longer operate between Cathedral and Meadowhall on Sundays.

Just over a year into the operation, the tram-train timetable was amended in December 2019. A small number of early morning services were withdrawn, with the third tram now coming into service from Cricket Inn Road to Cathedral at 07.28, giving additional time for vehicle maintenance. This means that between 05.27 and 07.27 the service from Cathedral is half-hourly. In the evening there are later services from Cathedral to Parkgate at 22.14 and 22.44. The last two departures from Parkgate are now at 22.51 and 23.16, giving a last arrival in the city centre at 23.42. On Sundays there are now only two tram-trains an hour, but services run later into the evening, half-hourly from Cathedral until 21.32 and from Parkgate until 21.04, two and a half hours later than was previously the case.

The journey time from end to end for the seven and a half mile journey is between 26 and 28 minutes.

THE TRAM-TRAIN ROUTE

From Cathedral, tram-trains, given route code "TT" on the front (rather than a colour – it is black on the Supertram map) follow the Yellow Route as far as Meadowhall South, serving all stops by request – this route was described earlier in this book. After Meadowhall South, tram-trains cross over the River Don and then turn sharply right onto the new 400 m Tinsley chord, firstly single and then double track before joining the former Great Central Railway (GCR) line (originally built by the Manchester, Sheffield & Lincolnshire Railway) from Woodburn Junction. This GCR line also parallels the Yellow Route tramway from Attercliffe and is used by freight and occasional diverted passenger services.

As the tram-train approaches Network Rail infrastructure on the Tinsley chord it activates axle counters that give a signal to Woodburn Junction signal box, which controls the former GCR lines at this point (eventually responsibility is planned to transfer to the York Rail Operating Centre), that there is a tram-train approaching. In both directions vehicles stop for around 20 seconds on the chord, as the driver flicks a switch in the cab to change from tram to train mode, or vice versa (in so doing activating the GSM-R equipment and changing the headlights from or to tram/train mode). Once the GSM-R radio equipment is live this gives the signal to Woodburn Junction signal box that the vehicle is ready to go and it is given the signal to proceed.

Heading north the line singles again to cross the River Don rail bridge before becoming double track. Tram-trains then pass the former steel mill in the Templeborough district of Rotherham, now rebuilt as the Magna Science Adventure Centre, to the right. This is a significant tourist attraction in the area, visited by more than 40 000 people each year, and shortly before this book went to press it was announced that Government funding had been secured to construct a new tram stop here. Also on the right, beyond the Bessemer Way road bridge to the right hand side, is the Templeborough Biomass Power Plant. The line then passes underneath the freight-only "Old Road" railway line from Chesterfield to Rotherham Masborough before joining the Rotherham Central passenger line alongside the CF Booth's scrapyard to the left. Almost immediately Rotherham United FC's New York stadium is passed on the right.

Rotherham Central

The tram-train then arrives at Rotherham Central station, where major changes have been carried out to accommodate tram-trains. The station here was built in 1987 (replacing Masborough as a station closer to the town centre) and modernised in 2012. The railway platforms have been extended to the south, with new low-height platforms at the south end to be served by tram-trains.

Parkgate

Leaving Rotherham Central it is then just over a mile to the terminus at Parkgate, with tram-trains running alongside Northern local services as well as some freight traffic. There is a short spur off the Rotherham–Swinton railway line on the west side to the single platform terminus with a short refuge beyond where a tram-train can be stabled if needed. The terminus is slightly further north than originally planned. It is a short walk to the nearby out-of-town Parkgate retail park, which has a number of shops and eating establishments and despite being in the shadow of nearby Meadowhall is visited by around nine million people every year. Initially a small Park & Ride site was established here with 32 spaces. In a significant development this facility was increased to 95 spaces at the end of 2019.

OPERATION

The service is wholly operated by Stagecoach Supertram. Initially, 24 drivers were trained to operate the tram-train service, and all also still drive on the rest of the tram network. The 24 drivers were drawn from a pool of Supertram drivers (all of whom volunteered for tram-train

work) that must have had a minimum of one year driving trams. There are eight driver rosters on Mondays–Saturdays and six on Sundays. All conductors were trained to operate tram-train. The small pool of drivers need to use a completely different style of driving, from line of sight driving on the tramway to driving under signals. Railway standards had to be incorporated into the Supertram rulebook; it should be remembered that Supertram and Network Rail are two very different organisations, with different standards and sets of practices. In total the project created 35 new jobs, 25 for drivers and ten for maintenance and revenue protection.

Potential future developments to tram-train are discussed in the "Supertram after 2024" section. Another possibility that has been looked at by Stagecoach is the extension of the service through to Shalesmoor, which would give Parkgate

Left: A sunny summer's early evening at Rotherham Central on 13 August 2019 sees 399 201 arriving with the 17.51 to Parkgate. **Robert Pritchard**

Below: 399 201 is seen again, leaving Parkgate for Cathedral on 13 August 2019. **Robert Pritchard**

more direct services, for example, to the University of Sheffield stop and would reduce congestion at Cathedral where Purple Route services already turn back. However, an extension to Shalesmoor would require at least four tram-trains to be diagrammed.

ONE MILLION PASSENGERS IN FIRST YEAR BUT PROBLEMS SURFACE

Tram-train celebrated its first birthday at the end of October 2019. The first year was not without problems, however, notably the two accidents damaging two vehicles, a number of incidents of flooding in the Rotherham Central and Meadowhall South areas and also some problems with the overhead power supply, particularly with ice forming on the overhead on very cold mornings. Following the discovery of a fault with a bogie-mounted bracket on one of the vehicles, tram-train services were suspended from the evening of 9 April 2019 whilst Stadler undertook safety inspections. Ticket acceptance was agreed with Northern trains and local bus operators, with a twice-hourly tram-train service reinstated from the afternoon of 10 April and a full service from the following day. Tram-train services were again disrupted in early June, with only two services per hour as the vehicles were progressively taken out of traffic for engineers to reinstate the vehicles' bogie covers, which were removed following the fault discovered in April. The third hourly tram-train service closely follows a Yellow Route tram in either direction and is said to be relatively lightly used. Whilst the vehicles were out of service Supertram advised that additional work was taking place to address some unrelated faults that had led to declining availability in the fleet. The full service was resumed from 12 June.

Worse was to come in the autumn: on 26–27 October and for ten days from 7 to 16 November 2019 the service was unable to operate at all owing to exceptional flooding at Rotherham Central, which completely closed the line to both trains and tram-trains. The Meadowhall branch of the tram network was also closed between Meadowhall South and Meadowhall for a week, with the River Don reaching the top of the bridge at Tinsley, putting the structure at risk. Tram replacement bus services were in operation during this time.

Above: 399 201 is about to cross the River Don and pass under Blackburn Meadows Way heading towards Cathedral on 24 March 2019. **Robert Pritchard**

Then on the evening of 13 December, Stadler grounded the tram-train fleet and the service had to again be suspended entirely. Stadler explained that the decision followed the discovery of a fault relating to a hydraulic unit on one vehicle. All seven units were consequently grounded as a precautionary measure so that Stadler engineers could establish the root cause of the problem and then work on a solution. A reduced service of two tram-trains was reintroduced from the afternoon of 17 December. The tram-train service had already been reduced to two services per hour for several weeks following modifications being carried out to the vehicles. The two-trams-per-hour service continued until 19 January 2020, with at least one other occasion when the service was completely suspended for several hours. Monday–Saturday tram-trains were operating from Cathedral to Parkgate at xx.00 and xx.27 minutes past the hour until 20.27, then at 21.07, 21.27, 22.14 and 22.44 and from Parkgate to Cathedral at xx.31 and xx.59 minutes past the hour until 20.59, then at 21.46, 22.16, 22.51 and 23.16. The full three-trams-per-hour service resumed on 20 January 2020, with 399 204 re-entering service the previous day. There was further flooding at Rotherham Central leading to the suspension of the tram-train service between 16 and 20 February 2020.

Notwithstanding these problems, as the pilot scheme approached its first anniversary, SYPTE proudly announced that it had already received its millionth passenger. This is in line with the original Stagecoach expectations – the business case had been built on one million passengers after the first year. At this stage, Executive Director Stephen Edwards said the DfT-funded trial has been "hugely successful", with customer satisfaction and passenger numbers both exceeding expectations. He added: "Our region is leading the way for tram-train learning and application in the industry. We're proud to deliver this important pilot locally, and to be part of the future opportunities the pioneering technology could provide, both for our region and beyond."

A Transport Focus survey (carried out before the problems with flooding and tram-train availability in the late autumn of 2019) found that 100% of passengers were satisfied with the overall tram-train journey and the journey times on the route. 92% of respondents were satisfied with its value for money, and 90% with the punctuality of services. Almost all other key measures scored over a 90% satisfaction rate. Despite the tight turnaround at each end, during the first five months tram-train achieved around 95% punctuality.

It is clear the tram-trains are proving popular with passengers from Rotherham commuting into Sheffield city centre (where the tram-train takes them much closer than the railway station) or for shopping trips. The tram-trains are quick and comfortable. It is also popular for journeys that were previously hard to make by public transport (without changing), such as Rotherham–Valley Centertainment, and also for workers at Meadowhall. One can be standing at Rotherham Central station in the early evening and see at least 50 or 60 passengers disembarking from a tram-train. However, there does seem to be significantly less patronage to Parkgate at certain times of day, and your Authors have sometimes been on a tram-train between Rotherham Central and Parkgate and been the only passenger on board! There has also been criticism about the lack of ticket integration, for example of all the various tickets available, only the more expensive South Yorkshire Connect+ can be used on both trains and tram-trains, and for someone making a return trip from Rotherham to Sheffield they must return via the same mode of transport if they buy a return ticket – some flexibility here would be good and would mirror what is common on the continent where multiple modes of transport operate on the same route.

WHERE ELSE FOR TRAM-TRAINS?

It has been beset by problems and escalating coats, but can the Sheffield–Rotherham pilot become a model for other urban areas in Britain? Although some operate over former railway lines, the seven tramways already in operation in Britain were designed in isolation, not to interact with the national railway network. A number of other transport authorities across the UK are observing the Sheffield–Rotherham pilot with considerable interest to help to decide whether the same concept could be adapted for use elsewhere. In particular, Transport for Greater Manchester is currently assessing the feasibility of testing the use of tram-trains on the Rochdale–Heywood, Manchester Airport–Wilmslow and Altrincham–Hale lines. If successful, these could pave the way for their introduction on other routes in Greater Manchester such as Rochdale–Heywood–Bury, Stockport–Manchester Airport, Colnbrook–Manchester Airport via Timperley, and the existing heavy rail lines from Manchester to Hadfield/Glossop, Marple, Hazel Grove, Warrington via Trafford Park, and Wigan via Atherton, TfGM believes.

Transport for Wales has also ordered Stadler Citylink tram-trains similar to those of Supertram as part of its South Wales Metro project, and these will be introduced on the Cardiff Valley lines in 2022–23. Some vehicles will also feature batteries as some sections, including tunnels, will not be electrified. This scheme envisages a number of potential new light rail and bus rapid transit-based routes linking existing heavy rail lines that are currently separate, and including some on-street running. The city of Bristol is also watching closely, with regard to the proposed MetroWest scheme.

Below: 399 206 crosses the River Don at Meadowhall South, which flooded here for several days in November 2019, with a service for Parkgate on 24 March 2019. **Robert Pritchard**

399 201 passes the "Trams Only" sign as it leaves Parkgate and joins the railway line to Rotherham Central on 3 February 2019. **Robert Pritchard**

Right: An access path was opened up between the Parkgate retail park and the tram stop (this path, alongside the Boots store, already existed but previously had a lockable gate at one end). **Robert Pritchard**

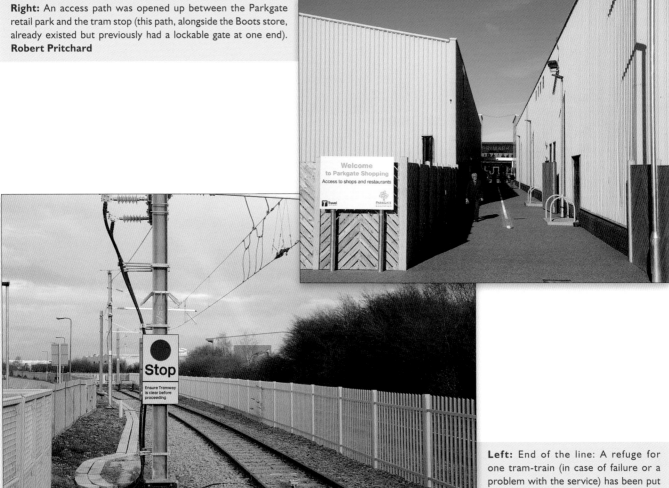

Left: End of the line: A refuge for one tram-train (in case of failure or a problem with the service) has been put in place beyond the platform at Parkgate. **Robert Pritchard**

PARKGATE PROGRESS

The Eastwood footbridge alongside the Sheffield & South Yorkshire Navigation Canal (Rotherham Cut) at Rotherham Parkgate provided a good vantage point to watch progress with the new tram-train terminus, a single-track spur off the main line. In these three images we see how things slowly progressed from 2016 to completion in 2018. In the top photo, taken on 16 August 2016, the site has been cleared and some track panels laid as DB Cargo 60007 "The Spirit of Tom Kendell" passes with a well-loaded 6J57 18.14 Aldwarke–Stocksbridge steel train, a train which runs daily on weekdays. In the middle photo, on 26 July 2017 track is laid into the new terminus with overhead supports starting to be erected. 66128 passes with the same train. The bottom photos shows the completed arrangement as Northern DMUs 144 013 and 153 307 pass with the 17.15 York–Sheffield on 13 August 2019. The footbridge itself received a new deck to raise it above the space required for the overhead wires. **Photos Robert Pritchard (3)**

THE STADLER
TRAM-TRAINS

The purpose-built CityLink tram-train vehicles were constructed by Vossloh Espana (now Stadler) at its works at Albuixech, Valencia, Spain, with electrical equipment from Vossloh Kiepe in Düsseldorf. They were based on the vehicle by the same supplier for Alicante's tram-train operation and also similar in basic design to the 25 cars ordered for the German tram-train operation in Karlsruhe. These are dual voltage vehicles – at 750 V DC and 25 kV AC – the latter equipment was tested in Spain before delivery to cater for any future electrification of the Midland Main Line north of Sheffield. As dual-voltage vehicles the process of switching between two voltages is automated. An Automatic Power Control (APC) system, which uses magnets embedded in the ground outside of the rail, separates the two power supplies with a neutral section of track. As the vehicle travels over the first magnet it triggers the circuit breakers to open. The tram-train then coasts through the neutral section before detecting the new voltage and closing the circuit breakers. Although it is automated, there is a manual override that would allow the driver to close the circuit breaker if needed.

The tram-trains were designed to be very similar to the original Siemens-Duewag cars as they would also be used on the conventional tramway and be required to fit in the same platforms as the original trams. They are made up of three articulated sections, and are slightly longer than the originals.

The cars have one bogie under each of the end sections and two under the high floor centre section. Each end section has the same layout with 22 seats plus four tip-ups and one wheelchair space. A single step leads to the middle section, which has 44 seats, arranged airline style and in bays of four, but the seats do not align as well with the windows as in the original trams, where all are arranged in bays of four.

Maximum speed on the tram network is 50 mph (only normally achieved between Meadowhall South and Carbrook) and 55 mph on Network Rail, although the vehicles are capable of 100 km/h (just over 60 mph). Unlike the Siemens cars not all bogies are powered – one of the four is unpowered, as instead the wheelsets are independently powered. The vehicles are fitted with the same type of emergency Albert coupler as the original fleet. As the tram-trains' centre of gravity is higher than the original trams, due to an extra 12 tonnes of weight (much of it roof-mounted equipment), a pneumatic secondary suspension system is fitted that also lowers the ride height slightly. Other technical information is shown in Table 1.

Seven tram-trains were built, tram numbers 201–207, and also, as they run over the national railway network, given TOPS numbers 399 201–399 207, which are carried on the front end (the three-digit numbers are carried in the traditional tramway position, above the cab door). To comply with Rolling Stock Library requirements, each section of the tram carries a railway-style six-digit number, in the series 999001–007, 999101–107 and 999201–207. The seven tram trains were to form two distinct fleets, because a different wheel profile is needed for running over the national rail network. Four trams were to be dedicated to the tram-train service with the other three supplementing the fleet of 25 Siemens trams on the existing system.

Above: At the end of its long journey from Valencia, 399 201 is delivered to Nunnery depot on 30 November 2015. **Paul Jackson**

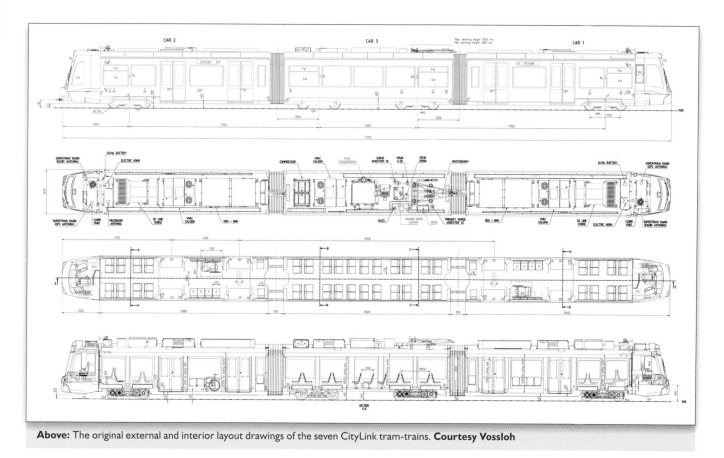

Above: The original external and interior layout drawings of the seven CityLink tram-trains. **Courtesy Vossloh**

All seven vehicles have, however, been fitted with the railway safety systems TPWS, OTMR and GSM-R (cab radios) as well as Supertram radios. TPWS is active at all times, but the GSM-R is activated as the trams pass onto the national rail network. It should be noted that Network Rail fitted TPWS to every signal on the route as an added mitigation for extra safety.

DELIVERIES AND SERVICE INTRODUCTION

The first set, 399 201, was delivered to Nunnery depot on 30 November 2015 having made the journey from the Port of Santander on the north-east coast of Spain to Southampton, and then by road to Sheffield. It was presented to local media and stakeholders a few days later on 10 December, with the then Transport Minister Andrew Jones in attendance to cut a ribbon to formally launch the vehicle. All seven sets were delivered within a year (see Table 2). 399 201 started overnight testing between Nunnery depot and Meadowhall during February 2016. It also visited all lines in the city centre during the week beginning 22 February, running on various nights to Sheffield Station, Cathedral and Shalesmoor. Weights were added for some runs to simulate a fully-laden tram.

Adorned with a large red bow and full Stagecoach livery, 399 201 is launched to the media at Nunnery depot on 10 December 2015. **Robert Pritchard**

TABLE I: VOSSLOH/STADLER CITYLINK TRAM-TRAIN SPECIFICATIONS

Built	2014–15 by Vossloh/Stadler, Valencia, Spain
Systems	750 V DC/25 kV AC overhead
Wheel arrangement	Bo-2-Bo-Bo
Traction motors	6 x VEM of 145 kW (195 hp)
Seats	88 (+8 tip-ups)
Standing capacity (4 per sq m)	140
Length	37.20 m
Width	2.65 m
Height	3.72 m
Entrance height	425 mm
Wheel diameter	720 mm
Min curve radius	22 m
Couplers	Albert (emergency use)
Doors	Sliding plug
Weight	64 tonnes
Braking	Regenerative, disk and emergency track
Maximum permitted speed	55 mph (on tramway 50 mph)

TABLE 2: STADLER TRAM-TRAIN DELIVERY DATES

Tram No.	Date delivered to Nunnery depot
399 201	30 November 2015
399 202	24 May 2016
399 203	28 June 2016
399 204	19 July 2016
399 205	26 September 2016
399 206	17 October 2016
399 207	20 November 2016

TABLE 3: STADLER TRAM-TRAIN FORMATIONS (REVISED AFTER THE ACCIDENTS)

Tram No.	Formation
399 201	999001 999101 999201
399 202	999002 999102 999204
399 203	999003 999103 999203
399 204	999004 999104 999202
399 205	999005 999105 999205
399 206	999006 999106 999206
399 207	999007 999107 999207

Above: Flanked by Northern Powerhouse and Tram-Train Project posters, Transport Minister Andrew Jones addresses the media at the launch of 399 201 as South Yorkshire PTE Executive Director Stephen Edwards looks on. **Robert Pritchard**

After a protracted period of testing, driver training started in early April 2017 and the sets first entered service on the existing network from 14 September 2017. 399 202 became the first vehicle to carry passengers in public service, almost two years after the first set arrived in Sheffield. Before running to Meadowhall with invited guests on board and then entering service, the tram was named "Theo The Children's Hospital Charity" at Nunnery depot by Rail Minister Paul Maynard. On the following Sunday, 17 September, 399 202 spent the day in "fund raising service" on both the Blue and Yellow Routes with passengers asked to make a donation to the Children's Hospital Charity, rather than pay a fare.

The type was initially mainly kept on the Purple Route but later used across all routes, although they are preferred on the longer Blue Route. During October 2017 all seven cars were used as trams, with tram wheel profiles, and some were later to be converted to tram-trains. As described in the previous chapter, tram-train services started on 25 October 2018.

TWO FLEETS

The situation at the start of the tram-train service was that 399 201–204 would be dedicated to the Parkgate service, with the slightly different wheel profile for tram-train running: Street sections of Supertram have grooved rails that cannot be negotiated by the broader wheel profiles that are standard to vehicles that run on NR tracks. Conversely, the wheels of the trams are not compatible with NR switch blades. 399 201–204 have tyre profiles known as S1 type and can be used to Parkgate and on city centre track that has been relaid; on the existing system to Meadowhall, Shalesmoor and Spring Lane. 399 205–207 had tram profile wheels for use across the whole of the tram system. A spare set of bogies with tram-train profile was delivered with the tram-trains to enable a car to be converted quickly to a tram-train if needed.

Unfortunately, the spare set of bogies were needed rather more quickly than had been intended after the accident involving 399 204 on the opening day, badly damaging vehicle 999004. As a result 399 206 was swiftly converted to a tram-train, leaving 399 201–203/206 as tram-trains and 399 205/207 as conventional trams. The further accident involving 399 202 just over a month after opening saw a hybrid formed using cars 999002 and 999102 from 399 202 and car 999204 from 399 204. This hybrid was given the number 399 202 and also the "Theo" name on vehicle 999204, as well as the original name carried by 999002. It re-entered service on 18 December 2018. The other three damaged vehicles were returned to Stadler's plant in Spain for extensive repairs and testing in February 2019. They were returned back to Nunnery depot on 17 November that year and entry back into service came on 19 January 2020. Vehicle 999202 in 399 204 still carries its own "Theo" name, so three end cars actually carry this name at the time of writing. It is not expected that the vehicles will be reformed back to their original formations, and at the time of this book going to press there are five of the Stadler cars passed for tram-train operation: 399 201–204/206.

Stadler is contracted to maintain the vehicles at Nunnery depot for the first two years of the trial and the contract calls for six of the seven vehicles to be available for service (although obviously the accident made this very difficult for the whole of 2019).

Left: The spare set of tram-train bogies that were delivered to Nunnery depot with 399 201. **Paul Jackson**

Below: On its first test run into the city centre 399 201 is seen on the run down from Hyde Park towards the Park Square triangle on 22 February 2016. **Paul Jackson**

Above: 399 202 climbs up to Hyde Park from the city centre whilst on driver training on 21 August 2018. **Paul Jackson**

Above: Underneath the sand and battery charge boxes is a small "tram" or "Tram Train" logo to indicate the wheel profile that vehicle has. **Robert Pritchard**

Right: The front ends of the Stadler vehicles look most different from the Siemens cars, being predominantly black rather than red. 399 205 leaves Granville Road/Sheffield College with a Blue Route service for Malin Bridge on 3 December 2019. **Robert Pritchard**

Left: Nunnery depot was adapted to take the additional trams in the fleet, including a new crane and extended gantries to access the roof-mounted equipment. On 13 September 2019 399 201 receives maintenance inside the depot. Since introduction the Citylink vehicles have received more than 100 modifications. **Paul Abell**

Below: A broadside view of the only named Sheffield tram: 399 202 "Theo" arrives at Rotherham Parkgate on 25 October 2018, the opening day for the tram-train service. **Robert Pritchard**

Above: The Theo nameplates applied to 399 202. **Andrew Dyson**

399 203 passes the entrance to the Supertram depot at Nunnery with a service for Cathedral on 29 November 2019. At this time only two tram-trains were in operation per hour due to modifications being carried out on the vehicles. **Robert Pritchard**

Above & right: Two views of the high floor centre section of 399 201, showing some bays of four seating, as well as some airline style seats – a notable difference to the original trams. **Robert Pritchard (2)**

Above: The cab layout of 399 201. To the right-hand side is the tram/tram-train switch that the driver turns on or off when on the Tinsley chord. **Robert Pritchard**

Below: The view looking towards the front of 399 201 showing the wheelchair space to the right. **Robert Pritchard**

WHEN THINGS GO WRONG

The tram-tram service suffered a number of overhead line problems in autumn 2019. On Saturday 30 November 399 203 failed at Ickles with the first Parkgate service of the day – the tram-train could not gain enough electrical current owing to ice on the overhead cables, so the pantograph automatically dropped. 399 206 was sent to the rescue but suffered the same fate and was marooned near Magna. Eventually, GBRf 66760 "David Gordon Harris" was summoned from Tinsley Yard to assist, the plan being to collect the two failed tram-trains and propel them to the Parkgate terminus where staff would work to re-energise the pair. At walking pace it took around 40 minutes to propel the vehicles from Ickles to Parkgate. The 66 left the tram-trains here and ran light engine to Doncaster. The tram-train service was suspended until the Monday, 2 December.

Above right: 66760 slowly propels 399 203 and 399 206 into the Parkgate terminus on the afternoon of 30 November. The raised checkrails over the points and crossing can clearly be seen.

Right: 66760 propels the tram-trains into the Parkgate terminus.

Below left: 66760 passes the Rotherham United ground at walking pace propelling 399 203/206.

Below right: The bar coupler used to connect the 66 to the tram-train. **Barry Clark (4)**

LOOKING BEYOND
THE EXISTING
NETWORK

In its first few years of operation, Supertram passenger numbers fell short of the numbers predicted, leading to a certain amount of uncertainty over the future of the system. However, by the beginning of the 21st century ridership levels were on the up and Supertram had become an established part of Sheffield's public transport network. Attention began to turn to possible extensions to the tram network. In the autumn of 2002 the South Yorkshire Passenger Transport Executive published ambitious proposals for six new extensions.

ROTHERHAM/MANVERS

It was proposed that a line to Rotherham and Manvers would leave the existing Supertram network via a spur just to the north of Meadowhall South tram stop on the route to Meadowhall. From there it would pass under the M1 motorway Tinsley Viaduct and take an alignment adjacent to the former Great Central Railway line almost all the way to Rotherham Central station – very similar to the route eventually taken by the tram-train some 15 years later. However, under the 2002 proposal, the tram line would have diverged to the right shortly before Rotherham Central, passing more directly through Rotherham town centre with a tram stop at Rotherham Interchange. The tram would then have continued on or alongside the main A630 road to Parkgate retail centre. The segregation of track alongside the former GCR railway line allowed for the provision of a greater number of tram stops along the route than has so far been possible with the tram-train, including at Magna, Bessemer Way and Main Street, adjacent to the railway line, and at Rotherham Interchange and St Ann's Road in Rotherham town centre. After Parkgate, the route would then have

continued along the existing Midland Main Line to Swinton and Manvers, a suburb of Wath-upon-Dearne.

WAVERLEY/HELLABY

This line would have left the existing Meadowhall line just past Nunnery depot and run along the former London North Western Railway branch from Wharf Street Goods to just beyond Woodburn Junction, then alongside the former Great Central Worksop line for a short distance before diverging onto the route of a branch line to the former Orgreave Colliery. This regeneration area, Waverley, gets its name from Sir Walter Scott's "Waverley" series of novels, which were reputed to be set in this area. The line could then have continued alongside the A631 road to Hellaby industrial estate.

TOTLEY/LOWEDGES

This line would have run south through the city centre, with a number of possible route options including via the pedestrianised streets of Fargate and The Moor or leaving the existing Fitzalan Square–Malin Bridge/Middlewood line after City Hall and then running along Furnival Gate and Eyre Street. The line would then have served Sheffield United football ground at Bramall Lane and then run alongside the Midland Main Line between Heeley and just past Millhouses and alongside Abbeydale Road South past Dore & Totley station to the terminus at Totley. The Lowedges line would have branched off the Totley line at Heeley, serving residential areas such as Meadowhead. A number of possible routes were considered, including the A61 Chesterfield Road itself, which is a former tram route but is also a major artery of Sheffield's road network.

In autumn 2002 SYPTE published ambitious plans to extend the Supertram network. One of the proposed extensions would have seen trams returned to Millhouses. Car 281 is pictured here on a dull day in September 1960, just a few weeks away from the closure of the route from Beauchief to Vulcan Road. To the right of the picture is a lovely selection of British-built cars. **Howard Turner**

Right: On 8 October 1960, the final day of operations on the first generation tramway, Roberts car 528 travels up Fargate. Since pedestrianised, Fargate was on one of a number of possible routes that the PTE's proposed line to Totley and Lowedges could have taken through the city centre.
Howard Turner

ROYAL HALLAMSHIRE HOSPITAL/ RANMOOR

This short branch would have left the existing route just before University of Sheffield tram stop at the junction of Upper Hanover Street and Glossop Road. Such an extension was also suggested in an earlier study in 2000 but would not have been viable on its own because of the high cost of a Transport & Works Act submission and the small number of additional trams required.

The preferred route was via Glossop Road, Clarkehouse Road and Endcliffe Vale Road. Two alternative routes were also considered: via Western Bank, Whitham Road and Fulwood Road or via the preferred route as far as the Royal Hallamshire Hospital then continuing along Glossop Road to Fulwood Road.

NORTHERN GENERAL HOSPITAL

This short extension would have left the existing Malin Bridge/ Middlewood line just before Shalesmoor and run along Rutland Road and Barnsley Road to the Northern General Hospital.

The lines proposed in 2002 followed a study carried out for SYPTE by consultants Oscar Faber and Parsons Brinckerhoff. Prior to this the PTE had carried out its own in-house "scoping study" to identify potential new tram routes. A number of routes were examined but rejected, including:

- Meadowhall–Waverley–Worksop.
- A circular route from Meadowhall via the Northern General Hospital and Shalesmoor using the existing tram line to Beighton then via Woodhouse, Waverley and the now closed Sheffield City Airport (now part of the Advanced Manufacturing Park) back to Meadowhall.
- A line from Stocksbridge via the Stocksbridge Railway Company's freight-only line to Deepcar, along the erstwhile Woodhead route to Middlewood, then joining the existing tram route and running to Nunnery then via Woodhouse and Beighton to Halfway.
- A line from Dodworth station, between Barnsley and Penistone, along the A628 road to just past Barnsley town centre then along the disused railway line to Manvers where a road alignment would be followed.
- A circular route from Shalesmoor via the existing route to Meadowhall then Rotherham–Manvers–Wombwell–Chapeltown–Parson Cross–Northern General Hospital–Shalesmoor.
- An extension of the existing Malin Bridge branch to Stannington.
- An extension of the Herdings Park branch to Meadowhead and Lowedges.

EXTENSIONS SCALED DOWN

In the spring of 2003, after the consultants presented the findings of their study to SYPTE, the PTE scaled down its initial proposals, with the line to Totley now being truncated at Dore and the Manvers line no longer continuing beyond Parkgate. The consultants found that a route to Stocksbridge would not be viable as there were not enough potential passengers to justify such a scheme, and claimed

that a line to Dore would attract around 5.8 million passengers per year but only 100 000 more if the route continued to Totley even though the proposed terminus of the truncated line at Dore & Totley station is right at the edge of the Dore and Totley residential area. The Lowedges and Northern General Hospital routes were also found to have lower potential benefits in terms of profitability, cost-benefit ratio and regeneration of the areas served than those routes that were selected for further evaluation. Under the 2003 proposals there would have been two new services: Dore–Hellaby and Ranmoor–Parkgate.

The PTE then carried out a detailed public consultation on these proposed new routes in the autumn of 2003. Public attitudes to the plans were assessed using a variety of methods, including questionnaire leaflets, an online questionnaire accessed via the project website, an interviewer-led survey of residents along the routes, and public exhibitions at five locations in the areas to be served. This found that there were high levels of support for the Dore and Parkgate extensions despite concerns about the environmental impact of the Dore route, particularly in terms of the on-street sections south of Beauchief. However, there was much less support for the Hellaby and Ranmoor extensions, with many respondents expressing concerns about value for money, disruption from construction work and the impact on residential and conservation areas. Some residents opposed to the Ranmoor route did support a shorter extension towards Broomhill, however.

Accordingly, by the spring of 2004 the PTE had cut back its extension proposals further. The Dore and Hellaby routes were abandoned altogether and the Ranmoor branch was cut back to run only as far as the Royal Hallamshire Hospital. Two route options were considered for the revised scheme: a branch from the existing University of Sheffield stop to the RHH, or a single direction loop via the Children's Hospital, Weston Park and Broomhill returning via the RHH.

In the event, even these revised schemes were not progressed any further, and in the summer of 2006 the Government asked SYPTE to work with the Department for Transport on alternatives to Supertram extensions such as a "Bus Rapid Transit" (BRT) based solution. However, documents released in late 2006 under a Freedom of Information Act request showed that the cost-benefit ratio for the proposed tram extensions was 2.06 but that of a BRT scheme was only 1.66. The released documents also revealed that the DfT had not completed its assessment of the value for money of the tram extensions before turning down funding for the scheme in its Regional Funding Allocation. A BRT system would have required a new dedicated route into Sheffield city centre, which would have added considerably to the cost of such a scheme. Alternatively if the BRT route were to run only between Meadowhall and Rotherham, passengers would have to change between bus and tram at Meadowhall.

Sheffield City Council's City Centre Master Plans of 2013 and 2018 both envisaged new tram routes across the city centre with the potential for extension to areas of the city not currently served (although without concrete proposals for any routes outside the city centre). In 2013 it was suggested that a second city centre route could run via Eyre Street, Cumberland Street and Charter Row, and in 2018 this was changed to a route serving Arundel Gate and The Moor. In either case such a route would relieve congestion on the existing line via Church Street, and would serve the new retail quarter.

Meanwhile, the Bus Rapid Transit North scheme was completed in September 2016. This involved the construction of the new 800 m Blackburn Meadows Way, a relief road opened in 2016 crossing over the Supertram line to Meadowhall and underneath Tinsley Viaduct, which carries the M1 motorway. This new road is also known as the Tinsley Link, and is open to all motor vehicles but has bus priority measures on the most congested sections of the route. Services X1 and X10 Sheffield–Meadowhall–Rotherham–Maltby, operated by First, run via this route, serving some of the same areas as the aborted Hellaby tram extension scheme. However, buses on this service take a more circuitous route than trams travelling via Darnall and Waverley would have done, and the journey from Sheffield to Maltby by bus takes around 1h7–1h9! Sheffield–Rotherham on this route is timed at 33 minutes compared to 27 minutes between Cathedral and Parkgate by tram-train.

On 15 April 1995 car 22 is pictured taking the sharp right turn at the junction of Glossop Road and Upper Hanover Street, on the approach to the University of Sheffield stop. The proposed extension to Ranmoor would have diverged here and continued straight along Glossop Road and up the hill towards the Royal Hallamshire Hospital. **Paul Jackson**

Above: At the Parkgate terminus on 13 August 2019 399 201 awaits departure for Cathedral as 142 063 passes with the 17.24 Adwick–Sheffield local service. **Robert Pritchard**

SUPERTRAM AFTER 2024

In 2018 SYPTE began work on a business case to fund the long-term renewal of the system post 2024. Ongoing maintenance costs are currently funded by Stagecoach; however, its operating concession comes to an end on 31 March 2024 and maintenance costs then become the responsibility of SYPTE once again. It has been estimated that some £230 million would be required to replace life-expired infrastructure and also the Siemens-Duewag tram fleet, which by this point would be more than 30 years old.

In preparing its Outline Business Case for the Sheffield City Region Combined Authority and the Department for Transport, the PTE conducted a public consultation between 24 September and 5 November 2018, with respondents being asked to consider three main scenarios for the future of the system:

- Maintaining the network as is: Essential work would be carried out when required to ensure that services could continue to run safely. There would be no investment to improve the reliability, frequency, or standard of service. Although costing a similar amount to the renewal of the system, expenditure would be spread over 30 years rather than being upfront. It is likely that this option would result in a lengthy period of disruption whilst works take place, and potentially a reduction in the quality of service over time.
- Renewal and modernisation of the system: Work on a comprehensive renewal of the track, power supplies, information systems and vehicles, as well as an extension to Nunnery depot to provide

Right: To promote the autumn 2018 public consultation on the future of Supertram, Sheffield City Region and South Yorkshire Passenger Transport Executive produced a leaflet detailing some of the system's benefits, responses to previous consultations and the various scenarios being proposed for the network after the end of the Stagecoach operating concession. For those without internet access this contained a questionnaire to be filled out and returned by post. **Courtesy SYPTE**

CONSULTATION ON THE FUTURE OF SUPERTRAM

MONDAY 24 SEPTEMBER - MONDAY 5 NOVEMBER 2018

Sheffield City Region

 **SOUTH YORKSHIRE PASSENGER TRANSPORT EXECUTIVE**

Replacement of the original 25 trams, now more than 25 years old, is likely to be high on the agenda once the current operating concession comes to an end in 2024. Still performing reliably and well-liked by passengers, on 29 November 2019 114 approaches Woodbourn Road with a Yellow Route service to Meadowhall. **Robert Pritchard**

TABLE 1: PUBLIC RESPONSES TO 2018 CONSULTATION ON THE FUTURE OF SUPERTRAM

To what extent, if at all, do you think that we should focus on maintenance and repairs to keep the current Supertram network continuing to run safely for as long as possible?	Respondents	
Strongly support	1262	43.7%
Tend to support	681	23.6%
Neither support nor oppose	314	10.9%
Tend to oppose	343	11.9%
Strongly oppose	203	7.0%
Don't know	55	1.9%
Not stated	30	1.0%

To what extent, if at all, do you think that we should look to renew and modernise Supertram to enable it to continue operating well into the future?	Respondents	
Strongly support	2117	73.3%
Tend to support	412	14.3%
Neither support nor oppose	85	2.9%
Tend to oppose	66	2.3%
Strongly oppose	114	3.9%
Don't know	16	0.6%
Not stated	78	2.7%

To what extent, if at all, do you think that we should explore other alternatives to the Supertram model?	Respondents	
Strongly support	200	6.9%
Tend to support	118	4.1%
Neither support nor oppose	159	5.5%
Tend to oppose	463	16.0%
Strongly oppose	1801	62.4%
Don't know	31	1.1%
Not stated	116	4.0%

additional capacity, would be started in 2024. Taking around six years to complete, this would mean that disruption would be over a shorter period of time than in the previous scenario, and would deliver the most benefit to Supertram users.

- Exploring alternative options: The tram system would be decommissioned, potentially being replaced by a dedicated high quality bus network. Modern, low emission vehicles (either electric or hybrid) would operate over the same routes where possible, and offer a supposedly similar quality of service to the tram system. With no track or overhead wires, ongoing operating costs would be lower, but the upfront infrastructure costs, which would include decommissioning the tramway and installing infrastructure for the buses to use, would be similar to renewing the tram network. It is thought that it would take around three years before the system would be operational.

Although only 2888 people responded to the survey (at the time of writing Sheffield has a population of over 580 000), their responses (Table 1) showed strong support for the continued operation of the Supertram system, with the majority saying they would like to see it renewed and modernised. 67.3% favoured maintaining it as is, whilst a small minority (6.9%) said that they strongly supported the last option. Almost 1800 people said that if the Supertram was to be decommissioned they would instead travel in and out of Sheffield by private car or motorcycle, thus adding further traffic to the city's already congested road network.

Speaking on the findings of the consultation, Mayor of the Sheffield City Region, Dan Jarvis, said that it was evident from the number of responses received that Supertram was a great source of pride and highly valued by those who use it. The renewal of the tram system is considered as being fundamental to the growth of the Sheffield region.

Sheffield City Region must now lobby central Government for the funding to modernise the system: further consultations on the future of Supertram are to take place once the Outline Business Case is complete.

TRAM-TRAIN EXPANSION

In July 2019 Sheffield City Region unveiled its Integrated Rail Plan setting out its vision for the development of the area's rail network over the coming years. The continuation and expansion of tram-train operations feature heavily. Under the plans the two-year tram-train pilot scheme between Sheffield Cathedral and Rotherham Parkgate would be made permanent. To encourage further usage additional car parking would be provided at the Rotherham terminus from 2021, whilst the following year a new stop and associated Park & Ride facilities would be opened at Magna Science Adventure Centre, between Rotherham Central and Meadowhall South.

Looking further ahead, in the medium to long term it is suggested that local train services, such as those between Sheffield and Doncaster, are converted to tram-train operation from the late 2020s. Being rerouted into the city centre over part of the renewed Supertram system, this would help relieve capacity issues at Sheffield station and allow Northern Powerhouse Rail trains between Sheffield and Leeds/Hull to be accommodated on the current infrastructure. It would also enhance connectivity and service intervals at Rotherham Central, Mexborough and Conisbrough. The services could later be extended to a new station at Doncaster Sheffield Airport. These proposals will be developed with Transport for the North as part of the NPR business case over the coming five years (2019–24). Sheffield City Region and SYPTE will also investigate the feasibility of opening new tram-train stops at Forge Way and Kilnhurst.

Longer term aspirations include the extension of tram-train services in Rotherham to Waverley and the nearby Advanced Manufacturing Innovation District, and also the Bassingthorpe Farm residential area. In Sheffield opportunities for similar expansions of the tram-train network will arise as the most appropriate mass transit solutions for the city's key corridors are assessed. Potential routes, some of which were previously considered for extensions to Supertram, include:

- Sheffield–Advanced Manufacturing Innovation District–Rotherham;
- Upper Don Valley–Chapeltown/High Green–Sheffield via Meadowhall, the Northern General Hospital and/or Hillsborough;
- Meadowhead–city centre;
- A north orbital line connecting Hillsborough to the Northern General Hospital, Meadowhall and the Advanced Manufacturing Innovation District;

- A new service to the south-east of the city from Handsworth, Woodhouse and Beighton, possibly including a spur to Aston and Aughton; and
- Improved direct services between west and south-west Sheffield, the city centre and the Lower Don Valley and Meadowhall.

The plans, which would revolutionise rail travel across the area if they come to fruition, have been welcomed by the Department for Transport; however, at the time of writing only the new tram stop at Magna has committed funding to proceed. A successful bid to the Government's Transforming Cities Fund resulted in a £166M award, part of which will be used to construct the new stop. There is no funding in place for any of the other schemes to be progressed with.

WHAT NEXT?

Clearly the Supertram system is now a well-established part of Sheffield's public transport network and has come to play an important part in meeting the city's transport needs, even if ridership figures have been well below original forecasts, and we would hope that it continues to do so for many more years to come. Passenger numbers held up well in the period 2007–11, despite the recession, and only started to decline during the track relaying work that followed from 2013 onwards. In our opinion closure and replacement with a bus-based system would certainly be a retrograde step, and this view would appear to be reflected in the 2018 public consultation responses shown in Table 1. Rather than contemplating closing the system, Sheffield surely must follow the lead set by other cities in expanding its light rail network. The use of battery technology, as in the West Midlands, could help facilitate a number of short extensions, to the Hallamshire Hospital for example, without the need for expensive overhead equipment, whilst tram-trains could help extend the network to other parts of the area, such as Stocksbridge or Woodhouse, using existing heavy rail routes.

Additional Park & Ride sites could also help to entice people out of their cars. We will continue to watch, and report upon future developments through the pages of **Today's Railways UK** magazine, with interest.

Above: Various extensions to the tram-train have been mooted, one possibly further north from Parkgate towards Doncaster. 399 201 leaves the Rotherham Parkgate terminus with a service for Cathedral on the opening day, 25 October 2018. **Robert Pritchard**

Above: Could a new tram fleet consist of vehicles similar to the seven Vossloh/Stadler tram-trains introduced into service from 2017? 399 201 is seen on test in the city centre on 21 August 2018 as it leaves Fitzalan Square/Ponds Forge. **Paul Jackson**

APPENDIX. ABBREVIATIONS USED

APC	Automatic Power Control	OCC	Operations Control Centre
BCR	Benefit-Cost Ratio	OLE	Overhead Line Equipment
BRT	Bus Rapid Transit	OTMR	On-Train Monitoring Recorder
CCTV	Closed Circuit Television	PTE	Passenger Transport Executive
DfT	Department for Transport	RAIB	Rail Accident Investigation Board
DMU	Diesel Multiple Unit	SCADA	Supervisory Control and Data Acquisition
EMT	East Midlands Trains	SCC	Sheffield City Council
ENCTS	English National Concessionary Travel Scheme	SPTS	Segregated Passenger Transport System
GCR	Great Central Railway	S/RLUTS	Sheffield/Rotherham Land Use Transportation Study
GTO	Gate Turn-Off	SYPTE	South Yorkshire Passenger Transport Executive
GSM-R	Global System for Mobile Communications-Railway	SYR	South Yorkshire Railway
LD&ECR	Lancashire, Derbyshire & East Coast Railway	TfGM	Transport for Greater Manchester
LRV	Light Rail Vehicle	TMS	Tramway Museum Society
MS&LR	Manchester, Sheffield & Lincolnshire Railway	TOPS	Total Operations Processing System
NAO	National Audit Office	TPWS	Train Protection Warning System
NR	Network Rail	VIS	Vehicle Identification System